JOHN

Collected P

JOHN THOMPSON

Collected Poems & Translations

Edited by
PETER SANGER

GOOSE LANE

Published by Goose Lane Editions with the assistance of the Canada Council and the New Brunswick Department of Municipalities, Culture and Housing, 1995.

Edited by Laurel Boone.
Cover photograph by Tim Crawford.
Interior and cover designed by Brenda Berry.
Printed in Canada by Gagné Printing.

10 9 8 7 6 5 4 3 2

Canadian Cataloguing in Publication Data

Thompson, John, 1938-1976.

John Thompson
Includes bibliographical references and index.
ISBN 0-86492-145-4

I. Sanger, Peter, 1943-   II. Title.

PS8589.H488A17 1995   C811'.54   C95-950246-7
PR9199.3.T46A17 1995

Goose Lane Editions
469 King Street
Fredericton, New Brunswick
Canada E3B 1E5

TABLE OF CONTENTS

STILT JACK

PART II

EARLY UNCOLLECTED POEMS AND TRANSLATIONS

TRANSLATIONS FROM RENÉ CHAR

LATER UNCOLLECTED POEMS AND TRANSLATIONS

it is the dead who sing. who is
to match their great chorus? I
bend to them in this graveyard at
Jolicure. only the flag on my
friend's plot waves. there is the
murmur of his voice. word after
word. there is no forgetting John.
whatever tack I take

Douglas Lochhead
High Marsh Road (1980)
Entry for November 27

John Thompson, December, 1974. Coll. SHIRLEY MANN GIBSON

FOREWORD

This book more than doubles the amount of John Thompson's work previously collected. The earliest of the poems in it were published in 1961 when he was twenty-three and completing the first year of a master's degree in psychology at Michigan State University. The last poem was scribbled mainly indecipherably on a scrap of paper which Thompson ground beneath his boot on a tavern floor. Two days later, on Sunday, April 25, 1976, Thompson died in Sackville, New Brunswick.

Like other admirers of Thompson's work, I welcomed Anansi's publication, in 1991, of *I Dream Myself Into Being: Collected Poems of John Thompson*, introduced by James Polk. But that publication reprinted only Thompson's *At the Edge of the Chopping There Are No Secrets* (Anansi, 1973) and *Stilt Jack* (Anansi, 1978). It left room for the present collection, which draws upon the persistent searching, preserving and sharing carried on by Thompson's literary executor, friends, former students, fellow poets and many readers since his death.

Where possible, I have collated the texts, using all published versions and Thompson's surviving typescript drafts and manuscripts. Among other sources, I have been able to use what Thompson in a letter called "my big black book of recent things" — his handwritten notebook of drafts. I have recorded the significant variants of the published texts, dated poems where possible, and made a few annotations on Thompson's more difficult allusions which correct or add to annotations published in my *Sea Run: Notes on John Thompson's Stilt Jack* (Xavier, 1986). As much as evidence indicates or a conservative intuition permits, I have attempted to present hitherto uncollected material in the chronological order of its creation. The Introduction offers much biographical information about Thompson which has not appeared elsewhere. It also modifies accounts which have appeared before (including my own) and suggests ways of hearing and reading Thompson's work within larger frames of reference than those provided by fragmentary anecdote or quenching deconstruction.

All but one of my acknowledgements for help are given at the book's conclusion as a kind of collective grace upon leaving. The exception must be the thanks made here to Shirley Mann Gibson, Thompson's publisher at Anansi, his intimate companion during the last three years of his life and his literary executor. She enabled me to work with many of Thompson's surviving papers. I am deeply grateful for her advice and help, though mine is the responsibility for any mistakes or wrongful omissions. She remains one of those friends of Thompson's who are addressed in the last couplet of ghazal XXXVIII.

Peter Sanger

INTRODUCTION

"I've been working in the dark . . ."

"There's no forgetting John." Douglas Lochhead, Thompson's friend, fellow poet and colleague at Mount Allison University, published those words in 1980, four years after Thompson died. Even for many who did not know him, Thompson dead persists in being a version of Thompson still present. As I finished editing this collection, he turned up yet again, in only the latest of a lengthening series of appearances in Canadian poetry and reminiscence, as "a mysterious poet (who I always thought looked in photographs as Grey Owl would have looked without his aboriginal drag) who also killed himself."

That is a description of Thompson according to Douglas Fetherling. Thompson deserves better. Trust poetry. Homages began appearing immediately after he died, written by Margaret Atwood (who edited his first book), D.G. Jones, Michael Ondaatje, Alden Nowlan, Douglas Lochhead and Phyllis Webb, to name only some of the best known poets. Thompson is at the party in "Claude Glass," the first section of Ondaatje's, *Secular Love*, where he is "one unhappy shadow" and the "friend who said he would find/the darkest place and then wave," an allusion to Thompson's ghazal XVI. Such a tribute, as permanent as such things can be, is part of the voicing of Canadian poetry, to be worked both with and against. Then there are, of course, the Thompson anecdotes. It seems that almost anyone who spent more than half an hour with him has one to tell: how he rigged up mountain climbing gear and rappelled down the side of his office building at Mount Allison; how he arrived, caked in ice, at a Mount Allison faculty party, having driven his old Volkswagen off the road and crashed it into a ditch. (He proceeded to thaw all over an Axminster carpet.) At another faculty party, he got drunk and destroyed a tomato aspic with his elbow. And there are various accounts of his threatening management of hunting knives: he liked to carve up tavern tables with them; he flourished them and uttered dark words, as James Polk said in a memorial essay. Herbert Burke, a friend and fellow-professor at Mount Allison, watched terrified as Thompson stabbed his blade into a tabletop. Madness, histrionics, or both? I am not sure if Thompson himself knew.

These and all the other similar stories can overlay Thompson's poetry in the same way that the same kinds of stories about Dylan Thomas, Theodore Roethke and John Berryman (poets admired by Thompson) threaten to overlay their work. Truth is, beneath the comedy or terror of many Thompson anecdotes, the logic and coherence of a profound man's difficult life were in play and played out. Despite such anecdotes of anarchy, Thompson was a meticulous, dedicated poet. He put himself through the discipline of a lengthy, diligent apprenticeship in writing and translation. He was also, at the deepest levels of his character, a moral, serious and loyal man who struggled to be faithful to those levels, despite psychological illness and chronic alcoholism. He did not always win this struggle and he sometimes hurt and frightened those who loved and befriended him. But he always eventually returned to a sense of responsibility for what he had done to himself and to others. That responsibility is at the root of *Stilt Jack*.

John Thompson was born to Harold and Beatrice Thompson (née Wilkinson), a first and only child, on March 17, 1938. Manchester, Lancashire, England, was the place of birth he usually gave out to friends, although he was actually born in Timperley, Cheshire, the county adjacent to Lancashire. His father died of a heart attack at the age of thirty-six, when Thompson was two. His mother, able to find work only as a textile millhand, could not look after him, earn a living and better herself. Thompson was sent to stay with an uncle, aunt and cousins in Manchester. His mother never did take him back into her care. She remarried later in life, becoming Mrs. Shanahan. In one of Thompson's university records, dated 1956, her occupation is given as "clerk" — probably a clerk-accountant. She and her husband emigrated to Australia. Thompson corresponded with her sporadically throughout his life. He did not forgive her for leaving him, but he was proud of her intelligence, ambition and accomplishments. No doubt his severance from her took place because of the conditions of survival in wartime, pre-welfare-state England; but whatever its rational necessity and factual justification, the absence of his mother caused Thompson grief and instability throughout his life. Yet Thompson's relationship with his mother was also one of the covert sources of his imagination. Like Trakl and Rilke, in various archetypal forms and screening figures, he invokes his mother's presence throughout his work.

Thompson spent most of his early life as a full boarder in a series of Manchester schools. At all times during this period he must have been under constant pressure to do well academically in order to continue his education. He entered Amberleigh Private School in 1942, at the age of four, and stayed there until 1944. Unfortunately, the school's records for this period have not survived. Between 1944 and 1949, aged six to eleven, Thompson attended Chatham's Hospital School in Manchester. I cannot trace this school; it apparently no longer exists. In 1949, Thompson passed scholarship exams which enabled him to attend Manchester Grammar School. Many of its standards, traditions and practices while Thompson was there resembled those of major private schools such as Eton or Rugby; and academically, Manchester Grammar, during at least the first half of this century, was considered to rank among the three or four best in England. (An approximate equivalent to it in Canada is Upper Canada College.) Manchester Grammar was founded in 1519. By the late nineteenth century it had acquired extensive charitable endowments from landed gentry and local industrialists and other benefactors which enabled it to enrol a large number of "free scholars," students of high academic ability whose families could not afford to pay fees for board, tuition and personal maintenance. Thompson was one of these "free scholars." His speaking voice (rather like Richard Burton's, but with a Lancashire rather than a Welsh burr), his dress and his manners struck some of those who met him later as aristocratic in their unpredictable combinations of polish and crudeness; they were the effects of a privileged education.

At Manchester Grammar, Thompson probably encountered the High Church Anglicanism upon which *Stilt Jack* draws. The only direct reminiscence of the period I have been able to find is Thompson's writing to a friend, "Sorry about my bad taste: at one time I played Haydn and Mozart quartets — lst. violin." One would like to know what poetry he read, whether he was taught by a master who knew something about current writing, whether he belonged to a literary or poetry club. In his earliest surviving poems there are hints that Thompson knew something about the English Surrealists, Apocalyptics and Neo-Romantics of the 1940s and early 1950s — poets such as Henry Treece, J.F. Hendry (who later emigrated to Canada and published a life of Rilke), Ruthven Todd and Nicholas Moore. Certainly, Thompson knew and admired the poems of Dylan Thomas, and I suspect he began to do so while at Manchester Grammar. Thomas, an inescapable figure by then for anyone interested in poetry, died in New York in 1953 when Thompson was fifteen. It is striking that Thompson, unlike many of his English contemporaries, does not appear to have been interested in the work of Auden or of poets such as Roy Fuller, Philip Larkin and Kingsley Amis, who set much of the tone of post-war British poetry. There are, in contrast, significant resemblances between Thompson's life, work and interests and those of Sidney Keyes, Alun Lewis, Keith Douglas and William Bell, all poets born some ten to twenty years before him. There is a common quality of formal elegance in their work deriving from classical and continental sources — Horace, Catullus, Vergil (all three of whom Thompson would have read and translated in school), Baudelaire, Rimbaud (from whom both Thompson and Douglas translated), Rilke and Hölderlin. Keyes and Bell were both, like Thompson, fascinated by Yeats's life and work. All were physically active men. Keyes, Lewis and Bell were, like Thompson, passionately committed to living out the romantic mythologies of landscape and the natural life. The least remembered now, William Bell, was, like Thompson, devoted to mountain climbing. And Thompson, like Keyes, Lewis, Douglas and Bell, often wrote elegiacally. They all sensed that something or other — call it the times or even call it themselves — had it in for them. They were right: Keyes and Douglas were killed in action during the Second World War. Lewis was reported killed in action in Burma, although there is evidence that he committed suicide. Bell survived service in the Fleet Air Arm and was killed by a fall while climbing the Matterhorn in 1948.

In 1955, aged seventeen, Thompson left Manchester Grammar after having obtained his General Certificate of Education in English, French and History. He could, at this point, have chosen to complete his obligatory two years of National Service in the British Armed Forces before entering university. This was the usual choice, but Thompson immediately entered the University of Sheffield as a private, not a scholarship, student. In June, 1956, he was awarded his Intermediate BA, ranking in Class I after being examined in economics, psychology and modern history. His highest mark was in psychology, which he chose for his honours degree concentration. His academic performance secured him scholarships for the next two years.

The 1955-1958 University of Sheffield calendars give almost no details about curriculum. It is clear from them, however, that Thompson chose a subject on the move. Between 1955 and 1958, the number of those teaching psychology increased from one, listed with the philosophy faculty, to three, who were listed under their own departmental subheading. One of the new professors was a specialist in industrial psychology. Rather than being Freudian or Jungian, the psychology offered was, I suspect, empirical, statistical and behaviourist. Its tone was probably set to a large extent by the logical positivism and acute but narrow linguistic analysis which then constituted philosophical orthodoxy in England. If that description is accurate (and it draws upon my own experience at the University of Leeds in 1961 and 1962), hindsight suggests that Thompson was working against his real grain, perhaps in an effort to understand himself, or perhaps (as Shirley Mann Gibson has proposed) because he chose to study what would exact an effort from him, an aspect to his character that appears in the precise, economical forms and language of his best poetry. But there is also some evidence that Thompson was able to read and think more widely and deeply than the bare-bones entries in the University of Sheffield calendars suggest. In May, 1959, the head lecturer in psychology, Dr. Peter McKellar, wrote to the education officer of the British Army regiment in which Thompson was then serving to request that Thompson be given help in "obtaining books and journals." The letter notes: "We have had a detailed discussion of Mr. Thompson's plans to proceed to a Doctorate degree on release from the Armed Forces. . . . Mr. Thompson . . . as a student, showed himself to be of high ability, and of superior intellectual calibre. . . . The subject he has in mind involves an examination of Nazi official psychology (which, I may add, because of its invalidity, made some contribution to the German defeat in the Second World War)." As the letter also carefully states, Thompson did well academically, graduating with a first class honours degree in psychology in June, 1958.

Between 1958 and 1960, Thompson served in 1 Wireless Regiment of the British Army Intelligence Corps. He was posted to Germany and spent tedious hours monitoring the disposition of some small unit in the Russian army. Ironically, his service ended in the same year as the National Service obligation; in any case, he belonged to a generation subjected from birth to intensive war propaganda and to the code of willing self-sacrifice. James Polk has written perceptively about the effect upon Thompson of serving in the army, but I think Thompson may have exaggerated his own activity as a roaring boy during these two years. When discharged, he was ranked as a Local Acting Unpaid Lance Corporal; if he was a roisterer, he was at least a careful one. I can add little to Polk's account except to say that Thompson's fluency with what the poet David Jones called the "efficacious word" was probably acquired during these years. He also may have been able to save his money to go to the United States. Gibson has said that Thompson spoke to her about the gratitude he felt for the friendship of an officer who noticed him reading a book of poetry, encouraged him to pursue his plan for graduate studies and helped him apply to Michigan State University in East Lansing.

Thompson enrolled at Michigan State in the summer term of 1960 as a master's candidate in psychology. He successfully completed the first year of his programme, then switched in either the spring or fall term of 1961 (existing records are not clear) to the Department of Comparative Literature. On June 23, 1961, Thompson married. His wife, Meredith Joan Marshall, the daughter of a University of Chicago professor, was also a student at Michigan State. She was nineteen, Thompson was twenty-three. In a letter sent to a friend about two years before his death, Thompson said he "began to write — 1960-61 or thereabouts." His own "carefully preserved manuscripts, drafts, unpublished poems and translations" of those and subsequent Michigan years were later destroyed in a house fire; but as best I can, working at a distance from Michigan with periodicals which have not been indexed in detail and which exist in broken sets even in the libraries most properly concerned with their preservation, I have recovered at least some, perhaps all, of the material Thompson published during his years of graduate studies, and I have included it in this edition.

The first published work was an untitled poem in French (I have titled it "La Cloche qui Sonne"); it appeared in *Michigan's Voices*, probably in spring, 1961. The notes on contributors describe Thompson as "resident" at Michigan State and the poetry editor of the new *Tarot: A Magazine of the Arts Published by the Students of Michigan State University*. The life of this magazine spanned only three issues in 1961 and 1962; Thompson was the associate poetry editor for the first two. The chief editor was future novelist Thomas McGuane (born in 1939), who graduated from Michigan State with a BA in 1962. McGuane was a close friend of future poet and novelist Jim Harrison (born in 1937), who had received his BA from Michigan State in 1960 and was at this point fairly erratically pursuing an MA in the Department of Comparative Literature. According to Harrison, "I sort of flunked out of the MA program"; but he received his degree all the same, after leaving Michigan State, mainly in recognition of the publication of his first book. Harrison's collection *Outlyer and Ghazals* (1971) was to be one of the key influences upon Thompson's

Stilt Jack. Thompson circulated copies of Harrison's ghazals among students in his writing classes at Mount Allison University.

Among the faculty advisors to *Tarot* were Hazard Adams, the Blake scholar, together with the man who became something of a surrogate father for Thompson, the Canadian poet, critic and anthologist A.J.M. Smith. Gibson has told me that Thompson knew while he was serving in Germany that Smith taught at Michigan State. He may well have learned this from the officer who helped him enter the university and may also have learned from the officer some interesting things about Smith which were to have a lasting influence upon Thompson's life and work.

In 1935, Smith returned to his position as instructor at Michigan State just after Theodore Roethke had left his instructorship there following a serious mental breakdown. Later, Smith was to become one of Roethke's close friends. Roethke called Smith "a very bright and amusing guy." He used Smith's poetry in courses he taught. The poetry of both Smith and Roethke shows markedly the influence of Yeats, with whose writing they both worked edgily, as did Thompson in *Stilt Jack*. Roethke's poem, "The Waking," one of Thompson's favourites, is quoted from, evoked and played with throughout *Stilt Jack*. It seems likely that Thompson listened carefully to Smith's discussions of Roethke as a poet and his stories about Roethke's life. Thompson would have learned about Roethke's friendship with Dylan Thomas, and such connections would have provided him with that sense of belonging to a poetic continuity which a certain kind of poet always hopes to find and prolong: Thomas, Roethke, Smith — analogues for Thompson's own life in England, the United States and Canada. Important also was Roethke's admiration for René Char, the poet Thompson was to write about and translate in his PhD thesis. Roethke's admiration was so intense that he told a psychiatrist he considered Char to be the elder brother he had never had, and then he wept. Roethke died in 1963, when Thompson was twenty-five. That same year, poems by both Thompson and Roethke appeared in *A Garland for Dylan Thomas*, a book of elegies honouring Thomas published by Clarke and Way in New York. Not only as a poet, but also as a Michigan native, Roethke had a large, devoted and knowledgeable following at Michigan State. By studying there, Thompson had placed himself in a matrix which was crucial in shaping his poetic imagination.

The second issue of *Tarot* appeared in the fall of 1961. In it Thompson published an elegy, "The Dead Lost on the Eiger," which is eerily reminiscent of the poetry and death of William Bell. The notes on contributors identify Thompson as "a divisional language and literature major" and "a transfer student from England." No records are available to prove this, but I believe these descriptions indicate that Thompson was taking senior undergraduate courses in subjects other than psychology in order to qualify as an MA candidate in comparative literature. He had taken no university courses in English, French or any other languages at Sheffield. It was not until June 9, 1963, following ten university sessions (including his first year of psychology), that Thompson obtained an MA in comparative literature. He proceeded to work for his PhD during the following three years. He supported himself and his family between 1961 and 1966 with teaching assistantships worth $2200 a year, which he supplemented by weekend work: fruit picking, commercial fishing, doing yard work, plastering, house painting, loading and hauling firewood, and office cleaning. Part time every term while he was studying and full time during the three summers when he was not, he did editorial work for Michigan State University Press. In 1963, he also taught a summer school session. Meredith worked part time between 1961 and 1963 until she was carrying their daughter, Jenny, who was born on May 14, 1964.

Thompson's literary achievements while he was studying at Michigan State, insofar as I have managed to trace them, were threefold. First, he published seven original poems and two translations from Rimbaud between 1961 and 1964 in campus or local publications. The most widely known of his poems at the time must have been Thompson's elegy for Dylan Thomas, "The Man in the Wind," which was published twice in periodicals before appearing in *A Garland for Dylan Thomas*. However, Thompson's translation of Rimbaud's "The Drunken Boat," published in 1962, is the best of the recovered work from this period. If read carefully and sensitively, all nine of the pieces can be seen and heard to prefigure and link up with Thompson's Canadian poems. "The Dead Lost on the Eiger," for example, anticipates "the roping down, / the last abseil" of ghazal XXXIV. "A Tale of the Moon" is latent with images for ghazals VI, XXIII and others; and "On Two Paintings of Van Gogh" prepares for ghazal VII in *Stilt Jack*.

The second literary achievement of these years needs more enquiry than I have been able to manage. As part of his editorial duties at Michigan State University Press, Thompson edited Richard Berchan's *The Inner Stage: An Essay on the Conflict of Vocations in the Early Works of Paul Claudel*, which was published in 1966. Berchan, a Belgian, taught at Vassar between 1955 and 1963 and then taught French literature at Michigan State. Among the acknowledgements in Berchan's book is this: "No special claims are made for the translations of the French passages; they are there to assist the reader in his reading of the original. I am particularly grateful, however, to John Thompson for his invaluable assistance in the translation of the poetry." Whether Thompson had hand enough in the Claudel translations to permit us to consider them his work, I do not know. I have been unable to trace Berchan. No copies of the Claudel translations have survived among Thompson's papers. Only a few in Berchan's book sound to my ear characteristic of Thompson's work. Something of his imagery, syntactical movement and rhythm does, for example, appear in:

> Sounds of men: footsteps, cries, laughs, calls, in front,
> Behind, songs, loves, brawls, bargainings, words!
> I want you blinded, O people moving within me:
> Be silent, sonorous spirit! Stifle yourself, mad voices.
> Sound of the sea! Sound of the earth! Sound of the wind!
> Murmurs in the dense woods; the bird sings. Frivolous

Days! Sleep, past! What do you still want of me, child?
Flower of this world, close up again your corollas.

And you also, heart, be silent! Be silent, sigh!
The old murmuring endures in me, and cannot cease.

But of more interest is Berchan's analysis in Claudel's early work of
conflicts between spirit and matter, between religion and poetry, be-
tween the operation of Divine Grace and the inspiration of the Muse
(Claudel's "*l'ivresse poetique*," which Thompson translates as "poetic
drunkenness," a primal energy in *Stilt Jack*). The same conflicts appear
throughout Thompson's work.

Thompson's third literary achievement between 1963 and 1966 was
his PhD thesis on René Char, with its one-hundred-page, seven-chap-
ter "Introductory Essay." This essay is Thompson's only critical
work. Following it are two hundred pages of Char's texts in French
accompanied by Thompson's translations. The Char thesis was not
just an academic exercise. Thompson's "Introductory Essay" fre-
quently reads more like a manifesto for the kind of poetic imagination
he himself believed in than objective, explicatory analysis. It is filled
with statements which are as much about the kind of poetry
Thompson wished to write and would write as they are about Char:
"The poem is always bound to the creatures and the elements, the
flowers and stones because they are the ground of being; and perhaps
because they rehearse their being so perfectly Char invests them with
sanctity and considers them as a moral paradigm. Wittgenstein has
noted what is precisely true for Char's poetry: 'Ethics and aesthetics
are one.'" "Nature is the home of the human, the divine, of Being, at
once and simultaneously." "There is in Char the same urge to reen-
vision life and things, as in Hölderlin. In both are the opposing wishes
to preserve and to penetrate the sacredness of things. For Hölderlin,
the poet is nothing if the gods are present, but his poetry is precisely
an attempt to restore life by restoring the gods." Throughout the rest
of his life, Thompson felt strongly about the central importance of

Char and believed in the value of his Char translations. One of the first things he did upon arriving in Canada was to send his thesis to Oxford University Press in Toronto in the hope that it might be published. It was rejected. In 1973, six years later, after the appearance of *At the Edge of the Chopping There Are No Secrets,* he proposed to Anansi that the translations be considered for publication. In a letter to Gibson he wrote that Char "is, for me, one of the great poetical powers of the century. It seems to me he should get the Nobel Prize." Unfortunately, funding agencies offered Thompson no tangible support because the project was not considered sufficiently "Canadian." (The fact that Char had a profound influence upon French-Canadian poets such as Giguère, Lapointe and Jean-Guy Pilon was ignored.) But in addition to their value and to Thompson's own confidence in their value, there is a further reason for reading his Char translations. They and Thompson's own poems are intricately and deliberately interrelated. Discovering those interrelationships is part of the joy of reading Thompson's work. Not only did Char's philosophical beliefs and the characteristic images of his work influence Thompson's poetry, so also did his brevity, swiftness and abrupt disjunctions that are faithful, nevertheless, to intuitive, inner logic.

Thompson received his PhD in comparative literature (with specializations in French, Italian and German) on September 2, 1966. During the previous fall he had registered with the Michigan State University Placement Bureau seeking a university teaching position. He gave Canada as his locational preference. The University of Calgary offered him one position, Mount Allison University in Sackville, New Brunswick, offered him another. Thompson told Gibson that he looked at a map and chose the Sackville position because it looked as though most of New Brunswick was wilderness. Another reason for his choice may well have been that he wished to be nearer to friends in Michigan, especially Smith, than he could be in Alberta. Thompson began as an Assistant Professor in the English Department at Mount Allison in the fall of 1966, at a salary of $8000 a year. He, Meredith and Jenny (by then two years old) moved into a rented farmhouse some four miles beyond Carter's Brook in Wood

Point, a long straggle of old farms, houses and cottages loosely spaced along the Cumberland Basin shore of the Bay of Fundy, some ten miles southwest of Sackville. It was in the house at Wood Point (not in the later one in Jolicure, as some say) that Thompson wrote the poems in his first collection, *At the Edge of the Chopping There Are No Secrets.* The idyllic, rapt quality of many of the poems in that collection conveys the happiness shared by the Thompsons during their early years at Wood Point. Until 1970 at least, theirs was an open house in the evenings and on weekends, where

friends, among them many of Thompson's students, met to eat, drink and talk. Every spring they dedicated a weekend to celebrating the opening of trout-fishing season.

Thompson published three poems, "Cold Wind," "Old Woman" and "Poem," during his first year in Canada. Stylistically, they differ radically from the Michigan poems. They are laconic, controlled, percussive. Their diction is stripped. Thompson had obviously learned something of these qualities from Char. He also had learned a great deal from William Carlos Williams, from Pound, and especially from Denise Levertov. At some point in his life, probably during the Michigan years, he met and liked her. He may well have known of and identified with Levertov's English birth and background. He admired her work greatly; I have been told that he used to carry an autographed copy of her poetry collection, *O Taste and See* (1962), about with him as a kind of talisman. He later gave this book to Gibson. It is only a coincidence, and a good example of the way that fresh possibilities in the language of poetry seem to impose themselves independently upon poets with the right gift for hearing at the

Wood Point house (1995). CHERI CROFT-WILSON

right time, that Thompson's new style recalls that of his contemporary, the English poet John Riley. Riley was born in Leeds in 1937, educated at Cambridge, and killed by muggers in 1978. He translated Hölderlin and Mandelstam, both important poets for Thompson. Working out of the same background of English neo-Romanticism, surrealism and American modernism as Thompson, Riley even occasionally wrote ghazals which show an extraordinarily close resemblance in their rhythm and syntactical movement, but not in their gist, to Thompson's own.

Thompson published very few poems between 1967 and 1969. I believe that this inactivity suggests that he was concentrating upon putting together the collection which became *At the Edge of the Chopping There Are No Secrets*. By the end of 1970, a large number of the poems in that collection had appeared in *Canadian Forum, Quarry, The Malahat Review, Prism International, The Far Point* and *Ellipse*, and had been broadcast on the CBC radio program *Anthology*. By the end of 1970 also, faculty and students at Mount Allison had divided into two groups. One group deeply believed that Thompson was a creative, generous, gifted, humane poet and teacher, often charming and funny, well-mannered, rather shy and reticent; his eccentricities of dress (he liked to wear woodsman's pants and a red and black hunting jacket under the dandified, reverse-conventional ragged black undergraduate's gown at convocations), occasionally rough language, hard drinking and uncompromising presence (or absence) should not be censured. The other group, smaller but administratively powerful and socially prominent, believed equally deeply that Thompson was irresponsible, academically dubious and pedagogically incompetent, a subversive and a failure as a writer, and that he should not be permitted to stay in the peaceable kingdom of this small, respectable university with its proper Methodist background. Consequently, in the fall of 1969 Thompson was informed that he would not be granted tenure when his four-year probationary appointment expired on June 30, 1970.

The events which followed this denial of tenure are too complex to be dealt with fully here. They are also still obscure because certain

Mount Allison files remain confidential. Thompson himself dispelled part of the secrecy by circulating his copy of a letter sent to him by the university's president, L.H. Cragg, dated April 4, 1970. The copy reads in part: "A University cannot responsibly offer to any person an appointment without definite term when there are serious doubts that he is the kind of person best suited to strengthen the Department and the University in general. . . . There are such doubts about your suitability for this University. Most of the tenured members of your Department entertain serious doubts about your potential." Four numbered reasons for denial of tenure follow. The first is that Thompson neglected his large first- and second-year classes, favouring instead his advanced class in modern poetry. The second cites "evidence of lack of breadth of interest and competence in the relevant field of scholarship, English Literature." The third criticizes "Your attitude to your colleagues and your apparent lack of interest and unwillingness to share in planning, developing and operating an effective programme in English." The fourth tackles Thompson's lack of "visible interest in the University, outside of your teaching and your association with particular students"; his "sporadic" attendance at Faculty Council; and finally his lack of "a substantial corpus of publications," a lack which, in President Cragg's opinion, made "requests for special consideration . . . as a poet" unacceptable.

Thompson countered this letter in a publicly circulated reply. He defended himself as a teacher by citing the evidence of course evaluations and of petitions signed and representations made on his behalf by Mount Allison students. He pointed out that his qualifications were "fully known on my appointment." As for as his absences from department and Faculty Council meetings, he noted: "I am not encouraged to join in planning the future with those who have excluded me from it." Thompson concluded: "I ask for no special consideration. I stand on my teaching at all levels and my creative work in poetry and translation — its value acknowledged by publication. In these matters — the primary considerations in judging the value of a faculty member in any university — I refuse to accept the suggestions that my qualifications, abilities (actual and potential) and interests are not suitable to the Department and the University."

The Thompson case was one of three situations troubling Mount Allison in spring, 1970; the other two involved the departments of education and home economics. All three impelled the student body to pass a resolution of non-confidence in the university's administration at a special meeting on April 5 called by the Mount Allison Student Council. Nearly seventy-five percent of the student body — almost a thousand students — attended. The students also voted to increase a student computation fee from $50 to $60 in order to pay Thompson's salary as a poet-in-residence during the next academic year if he was not reinstated.

The Mount Allison Faculty Association held a special meeting to consider Thompson's case on April 8, 1970. Six of the ten other members of the English Department (John Barry, Alan Bishop, Herbert Burke, Douglas Campbell, George Crawford and Wayne Tompkins) presented a statement of support for Thompson. Its third paragraph reads in part: "we emphasize that in our judgement the loss of Dr. Thompson would be serious. We believe that he has demonstrated brilliance. Such people are certainly too rare to discard for any but the most grave reasons. No one here is less likely to disrupt the Department; no one here is more likely to bring distinction to it." After a lengthy discussion (the special meeting began at 7:45 p.m. and ended at 12:30 a.m.), those present agreed by a secret vote of 50 to 2 with a motion which defended Thompson as a teacher, as a poet and as one whose "interests and abilities are especially valuable to this academic community." The motion asked that the denial of tenure be revoked and that Thompson's probationary appointment be extended "by two years without prejudice." Such, in effect, is what happened. In November, 1971, his appointment with tenure was approved by the appropriate committee.

There seems little doubt now that the Mount Allison administration handled Thompson's case ineptly. It misjudged the loyalties of many of his students and colleagues and underestimated their appreciation of his gifts. What can be said in the administration's defence is that from its point of view Thompson was a difficult, awkward man who refused to compromise and did not suffer fools as gladly as those who contract to work in a university usually find they must. There were colleagues who warned him in 1969 that his tenure was likely to be denied. They counselled him directly, or indirectly through mutual friends, to make some fairly minimal placatory gestures — such as, for example, attending meetings. Thompson refused.

As for his teaching, the evidence I have seen indicates that he usually worked conscientiously until 1973, when illness, personal difficulties and intensifying alcoholism progressively affected him. At his best — and he could be at his best in flashes even right at the end of his life — he inspired students who had never given or expected to give poetry any more attention than the curriculum required to passionate interest. At his worst, he offended some students by unpredictable absences, by cancelling classes for trivial reasons and by lack of preparation. He could be indulgent to his students, but he often showed rigour, even anger, when he felt that they demeaned poetry or took it for granted. He believed in the authority of great poets and exemplary poems. He emphatically told students in one class in 1968 that they had to know their Bible if they were going to write poetry. His retort and corrective to the trivial poem one student threw off for a creative writing assignment was a passionate reading of one of Wallace Stevens's poems. The small Mount Allison English Department expected flexibility and range of Thompson. Among other courses, at one time or another, he taught The Novel; Renaissance Non-Dramatic Literature; Canadian Literature; Victorian Literature; Modern Poetry; Advanced Writing; and a survey course, Chaucer to Pope. He also served as faculty advisor for several years to the students who produced the Mount Allison literary annual, *First Encounter*, in which five of his uncollected poems were published. During the last year of his life, he was preparing to teach Romantic Poetry, preparations which left some trace in *Stilt Jack*. Additionally, during 1973-1974, he taught a course in creative writing for inmates of Dorchester Penitentiary, a few miles from Sackville. He was proud of this course, done at his own volition without any official arrangements involving Mount Allison. The course was popular and respected. Many of the students developed a close bond with Thompson, whom they admired and trusted.

Anansi published *At the Edge of the Chopping There Are No Secrets* in 1973. Creatively, at this point Thompson was at the height of his power. In the early fall of 1973 he started writing the first ghazals of *Stilt Jack*. Particularly at the beginning, he wrote so quickly and intensely that it would be hard to say whether he created the ghazals or whether they possessed him. As he wrote in a discarded draft of the Preface to the book, he was "working in the dark with the poems — but why not?" Throughout *Stilt Jack*, Thompson is conscious of that ambiguity of possession and its mix of positive and negative implications: "words swarm on the back of my hand. / I don't run, // thick with honey / and sweet death // I love to watch the trout rising / as I fall, fall" (ghazal XXII). The ghazals were capable of "swallowing everything" (ghazal XXIII) — including their creator. Thompson in conversation and letters used to call the poems "guzzles," which, he claimed, represented a truer pronunciation than the spelling "ghazals." His pun, I suspect, was more sinister than some of his friends realized.

The first five ghazals were finished between September 23 and September 29. Ghazal II refers to the Thompson family's move from the rented Wood Point farmhouse (which the owners, the Tower family, wanted to reoccupy) to another old farmhouse with two ramshackle shed barns at the very small, scattered settlement of Jolicure, some five or six miles northeast of Sackville on the Tantramar Marsh. The house was bought partly with money loaned by Thompson's mother-in-law in the United States. In October, the Thompsons completed their move, and during the ensuing two months, in a house where, according to ghazal II, "we might be happy," Meredith and John found it impossible to live together any longer.

After the tenure controversy of 1969-1970, friends of the Thompsons had noticed signs of strain in their marriage. Guardedness between

John and Meredith also entered their transactions with the larger world. The house at Wood Point was no longer an open house. There were rumours of violent quarrels. One of the things which finally broke the marriage was the very move Thompson hoped might save it. The Jolicure house was isolated and separated from Sackville for part of the distance by dirt roads which could, in wet weather, be almost vindictively bad. The house was also in need of major renovations which Thompson had not the interest, skill, patience or time to carry out. Nor was there enough money to hire someone to do all of them. Optimistically, he had gutted the house of interior walls in preparation for reconstruction which was never started. The house was surrounded by huge, flat, open hay and corn fields. When the fall winds began, it offered almost no resistance to the cold.

Throughout October and November, Thompson taught, drank and quarrelled with Meredith, and drove himself through ghazal after ghazal; by early December he had written more than a dozen. At that point he flew to Ontario. He had been asked to read at Carleton University in Ottawa on a Friday. On Saturday he travelled to Toronto to meet the staff of Anansi Press.  Shirley Mann Gibson held a small party at her home in his honour. That Toronto party was the one James Polk has described in the essay prefacing *I Dream Myself Into Being*. During it, Thompson "gave short shrift to our polite questions, and began to bark out insults into the embarassed silence about mean publishers and a gutless Toronto literati that did not understand or value poetry. After less than an hour of this, the guests began to slip away." This kind of talk was characteristic. About a year after the party, in a letter to a friend, Thompson wrote about the possibility that he might become

Jolicure house, fall 1973. John Thompson is holding a copy of
At the Edge of the Chopping There Are No Secrets. Coll. SHIRLEY MANN GIBSON

a book reviewer and "take a crack at the typically unquestioned, revered, Canadian Literature establishment. Especially the mediocre hustlers." But other matters besides his truculence about literary standards influenced his behaviour. One was the impending collapse of his marriage. Another was that during the weekend of the party there began a physical and emotional relationship between Thompson and Gibson which enters *Stilt Jack* with ghazal XIV.

Thompson sent that ghazal to Gibson after returning to Sackville. By the middle of December, Meredith and he had separated. Meredith returned to the United States, taking nine-year-old Jenny with her. Thompson then started to endure what he later described in a letter as "a severe winter in circumstances which could only be called atrocious. At one point I was taken to a doctor in Sackville for a physical

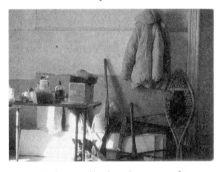

check-up, and he told me that I was 'physically and emotionally destitute.'" The physical destitution was caused by a frigid house, poor eating and excessive drinking. The emotional destitution was caused by the collapse of his marriage, his loneliness, the strain of his creative activity, and, above all, the absence of Jenny, which became the source of much of the despair and self-recrimination in *Stilt Jack*. She is one of the female presences, spoken to or spoken about, in the ghazals.

By June, 1974, Thompson had managed, at a slower pace than before, to bring the completed number of ghazals to twenty-five. Before leaving Wood Point in the previous fall, he had applied for a Canada Council Arts Award and a Canada Council Leave Fellowship. He obtained both and arranged to take a sabbatical during the fall and winter terms of 1974-1975. He planned to complete *Stilt Jack* and

Jolicure, winter, 1974. Tobin is leaning against
the wall. Coll. SHIRLEY MANN GIBSON

carry out research, not upon the French surrealists as one might have expected (and as I was told and reported in 1986), but upon "the influence of 19th century French poetry and prose on the poetry and poetics of Ezra Pound." (I quote from the rough draft of a curriculum vitae Thompson composed in 1975.) He decided to spend his sabbatical in Toronto. During the summer of 1974, he moved there to live with Shirley Mann Gibson and her two teenage sons.

I find it difficult to write about Gibson and Thompson. Gibson has suggested I do so clearly, without any of the careful vagueness of earlier writers on Thompson. But read together with *Stilt Jack*, hers could be the only truthful account. They had been exchanging letters for two years as publisher and author before they met for the first time at the party in Toronto in December, 1973. When they met they shared that sense of foreknowledge of each other at the profoundest levels which only those who have experienced it can understand, the kind of foreknowledge which can eventually kill those who betray it. After Thompson's death, Gibson published an elegiac sequence, "Tantramar Poems," in *The Tamarack Review* (Spring, 1980). The last poem in the sequence reads:

It is not easy to wake
place one foot upon the floor
force muscles to move
lurch into an unknown day.

If the sun shines
it will shine.
If not, it will shine tomorrow or
some other day.

Should I care that seasons change
months slip by
my sons grow tall
friends shelter me with their love?

I am beautiful for strangers
share laughter
speak with grace and guile.
That part of me which you possessed
keeps silent.

As for Thompson, initially his love for Gibson and the stability of
their relationship enabled him to try and recast his life with some
optimism. His health improved. He began controlling his alcoholism.
But his self-destructiveness was only tenuously in abeyance. Eventu-
ally, as Gibson has said, Thompson's sabbatical year in Toronto
became "fraught with disaster and trauma."

His research on Pound probably never even really began; at least,
nothing exists to show it did. I doubt whether the research was ever
a serious matter for Thompson, although a close reading of Pound
is evidenced in the parataxis and lyricism of *Stilt Jack*. Thompson
always diverted his scholarship into imaginative creation. No more
seriously tackled was a project to translate Aquin's *Trou de Mémoire*
which Anansi was prepared to consider for publication. Nor was *Stilt
Jack* completed. Evidence is that by the spring of 1975 there remained
six more crucial ghazals to be written. The general cause of
Thompson's difficulties was the accumulated burden and intensity
of the stress his life had subjected him to and the consequences of
ways he had chosen or improvised to cope with it. The tension and
losses of his childhood; the strain of succeeding in the impatient,
class-ridden meritocracy of English schooling in the 1940s and
1950s; the brutality, stupidity and boredom of his military service in
Cold War Europe; the cultural displacements he was compelled to
adjust to in the United States and Canada; the ambivalent profes-
sional situation he had partly created for himself at Mount Allison,
together with the collapse of his research plans; and the break-up of
his marriage, its financial cost, and, most of all, the loss of Jenny —
all weighed without relief upon him.

There was one further misfortune. On Wednesday, September 25, 1974 (a date confirmed in the October 2 issue of *The Sackville Tribune-Post*), while Thompson was in Toronto, the Jolicure house burned to the ground. It is said the fire accidentally started in woodwork which had been left smouldering by workmen who were carrying out renovations and had been using a propane torch. But the Tantramar Marsh that September was a place of mysterious fires. Three barns burned down, including one discovered by firemen early in the morning of September 26 as they were returning from the Thompson conflagration. Thompson lost almost everything, except what he had taken to Toronto in his Volkswagen. Most of the material which would have been part of his archive was destroyed — manuscripts, typescripts, notes and most of his books. Lost also were personal things — photographs, letters, mementoes — which had helped anchor him, an almost anchorless man. Although Thompson tried to deal philosophically, even flippantly, with the catastrophe for the sake of others, he was finally broken. At one point that autumn, after the fire, he experienced an episode of uncontrollable paranoia which led to two weeks' treatment in the Clarke Institute of Psychiatry in Toronto. He reached a state where he became a frightening presence in Gibson's home. From late 1974 until his death in April 1976, Thompson was increasingly subject to massive depressions, which rendered him nearly catatonic, followed by outbursts of manic activity, during which he would lose that control over alcoholism which he tried desperately to impose until the very last month of his life.

Thompson returned to teach at Mount Allison in the fall of 1975. By now, he and Meredith were divorced. He took an upstairs apartment in an old house at 65 Bridge Street in Sackville. On October 18, he wrote ghazal XXI, the last ghazal to be entered in the big, black notebook of drafts and final versions which he had started in September 1970 with a draft of "If Our Arcs Touch." On October 29, he made out his Last Will and Testament, writing with a nibbed pen in the beautiful, clear, semi-printed script he always reserved for the final copies of poems. He had it properly witnessed. He had already discussed the clauses of the will with Gibson. Two in particular show his state of mind. Clause 8 reads: "All mountaineering equipment, compasses, hunting and fishing tackle, sleeping bags, down jacket, axes to be buried in the earth with me: in the event of my body not being found, these items to be buried alone without me." Clause 9 reads: "I request burial in the earth in a plain wood coffin." That last phrase recalls the "pine box" of ghazal VI, written more than two years earlier on September 30, 1973.

He must have hoped for some release from almost constant depression during a Christmas visit of Gibson, his daughter Jenny and a Canadian friend of Jenny's. He had last seen Jenny in Michigan during Christmas, 1974. Their meeting had been, to use his own word, "joyful." But it was emotionally loaded by the unhappy relationship between Thompson and Meredith. He would have hoped that seeing Jenny in Sackville might be free of such strain. But although he was able to write the lovely, gentle and optimistic lines of ghazal XXXVI on December 12, Thompson found it impossible to sustain the balance and coherence it proposes throughout Christmas. On Christmas Day, he could get up only long enough to sit numbly through Christmas dinner. Then he stumbled back to bed.

He did not teach the full winter term of 1976. For most of the first three months of the new year he was hospitalized in Sackville undergoing a heavy regime of drug therapy. A number of people know portions of what happened during these months and the concluding April of Thompson's life. Like Dylan Thomas when he was in similar straits, Thompson confided in many and sought help and advice from them. Not all of those he wrote to, spoke with and telephoned realized that they were not his only confidants. When Thompson died, there were some (and remain some) who felt the unshareable guilt of thinking that each alone, had he or she responded to Thompson rightly, could have prevented his death. Some of those I have talked to about the last weeks find recalling them unbearable. The exact sequence of the final events in Thompson's life is difficult to work out for these reasons. Nor, nearly twenty years later, can people often remember days and dates clearly.

While he was in the Sackville hospital several of his friends, particularly Herbert Burke, faithfully visited Thompson. They found him unresponsive, almost speechless, until the end of March, when his condition seemed considerably improved by the prescription of a newly available drug which Thompson's psychiatrist decided to try. As a result, Thompson was discharged, with the warning, almost wilfully naive in retrospect given his history, that he must avoid alcohol. When considering what happened in the ensuing weeks, one must remember that Thompson was not only continuing the night-sea journey of mind and spirit which had begun with his childhood in England, but also that he was the victim of unpredictable, misapprehended and interconnected physical conditions whose symptoms were behavioural and only partly within his control.

Immediately after discharge, Thompson moved by invitation into Herbert Burke's house. At first, he was settled and sober, but before the end of his first week there he started drinking again, perhaps as the result of a celebratory visit by a friend. Thompson was also still taking the new medication. His behaviour compelled the Burkes to ask him to leave. Thompson returned to his upstairs apartment on Bridge Street. There, in the evening, probably towards the end of the first week in April according to Wayne Foley, who was Sackville's Chief of Police at the time, Thompson fired one of his two shotguns into the air in the back yard while he was drunk. A neighbour lodged a complaint. A court order was issued, and Chief Foley entered Thompson's apartment on a warrant while Thompson was absent and seized both of his guns. Thompson tried to regain possession of them at a court hearing for which he hired a lawyer. He lost. The guns were confiscated and Thompson was prohibited from owning weapons for the next five years.

This incident was the source of two of the most extravagant anonymous stories still circulating concerning Thompson. One tells that he shot at or over the house of the university's president, the other that he shot the town clock. The first is obviously a crude, fictitious climax to the tenure controversy of 1969-1970. The second story is slightly more subtle. Its grain of truth is that Thompson really did hate the town clock's dominating proclamation of the virtues of calculation. The story also makes an implicit commentary upon one of the characteristics of Thompson's poetry which, like Satie's *Gymnopédies*, transforms events in quotidian time into occasions of ritualized perception.

At the mundane level, confiscation of the guns must have been humiliating to Thompson, compromising his self-wrought and hard-earned characterization of himself as a competent outdoorsman. Hunting ducks and geese on the Tantramar Marshes around Sackville had been one of his chief pleasures every autumn. Now that was gone. He was also deprived of one of his dearest possessions: the rare, beautiful,  semi-antique, double-barrelled box-lock twelve-gauge made by Tobin which appears in ghazal XVI and which he had asked to have buried with (or without) his body in his Last Will and Testament. Those who hate guns and hunting may find it impossible to sympathize with Thompson's attachments and probable feelings at this point. But without those attachments and feelings, Thompson could not have written poems like "On the Tolar Canal," "Norman Tower's," "The Narrow Road," "Partridge" — or (I find the list growing too long) many others. Kafka's fragmentary story, "The Hunter Gracchus," and Char's "Lascaux" sequence (which Thompson translated and profoundly admired) are analogous in intention to these poems.

Thompson telephoned Gibson, who was still living in Toronto, shortly after the middle of April. He told her nothing about the gun incident and subsequent confiscations and prohibition. He asked if

Jolicure, winter, 1974. John Thompson with Tobin.

he might visit her. At first, she was relieved to hear him sounding, in her words, "alive, alert and joyous again." Then she realized what he straightaway confirmed. Thompson was drunk. Protective of her family, frightened of his lack of self-control and knowing she had no further resources with which to help him while he was drinking, she would not agree to the proposed visit. Thompson cursed her and hung up.

He continued drinking steadily. At this point surviving evidence and collaborative testimony make it possible to provide days and dates. On Thursday, April 22, Thompson visited his friend Ross Galbraith, who lived at Point de Bute, a few miles from the burned-out foundation of Thompson's house in Jolicure. At Galbraith's home, Thompson wrote ghazal XXXVIII. He headed the ghazal with that number, adding an exclamation mark. He left what he designated a "holograph" of the poem with Galbraith. On Friday, April 23, Thompson spent part of the evening with two of his students at the Tantramarsh Club in the student union building at Mount Allison. It was there and then that he drunkenly wrote, threw on the carpet and spurned with his boot the fragmentary and mainly illegible text which has some notoriety among readers of Thompson as the "missing ghazal." The text was retrieved and kept by Akis Patapiou. After Thompson left the club, while driving erratically homeward, he was stopped by the Sackville police, taken to the station house and charged with impaired driving. He spent the night in jail drying out — not for the first time. Police records no longer exist, but Chief Foley (now retired) remembers the Friday arrest as only the last of several similar recent occurrences which were to be considered in court on the following Monday. Patently guilty as he was, Thompson would have received at least the then-standard penalty of a three-month suspension of his driver's licence.

Released on Saturday, April 24, Thompson telephoned Gibson in Toronto in the mid-morning. Speaking calmly, he admitted that he was unable to stop drinking, that he could not exist without "joy and celebration in my life." He spoke about some of the objects in his Sackville apartment and asked Gibson to make sure they would eventually be given into the right hands. He ended their conversation by advising her lovingly about her own life and the upbringing of her sons.

Thompson then spent some time with Douglas Lochhead in Amherst, Nova Scotia, about twelve miles from Sackville, where they ate lunch together. Thompson gave Lochhead his final but incomplete typescript of *Stilt Jack*, instructing him to forward it to Gibson. It lacked ghazal XXXVIII and a small number of other ghazals which Thompson had circulated, numbered as they are in the published text, in letters to friends and editors. Lochhead and Thompson drove back from Amherst in separate cars, and Lochhead remembers watching Thompson pass a truck with suicidal verve on the shoulder of the highway. I have heard that later in the day Thompson was asked to leave a home in Sackville because of unmanageable behaviour. He returned to his apartment on Saturday evening. Late that night, tenants in the apartment below heard muffled chokings and cries. Thompson's apartment was entered, and he was discovered either comatose or dead. He was taken by ambulance to the Sackville hospital where he was pronounced dead on arrival.

An autopsy indicated that he probably choked to death after drinking too much and ingesting the pills which had been prescribed to alleviate his mental condition. Perhaps his system could have resisted the consequent insults, but it was undermined, as was also discovered during the autopsy, by pneumonia. The autopsy did not provide conclusive evidence that Thompson killed himself. Whether he did or not, he had obviously prepared himself for death and, at the very least, put himself in death's way. Many of his actions, beginning with discussion of the clauses of his will and concluding with giving the *Stilt Jack* typescript to Lochhead, were part of a series of farewells.

On April 27, at 4:00 p.m., Thompson's funeral was held at St. Anne's Anglican Church in Westcock, not far from Thompson's former Wood Point home. Mount Allison University offices were closed at 3:00 p.m. I have been told by several people of the great sadness shared by students and many faculty when Thompson's death became known. There was also a strange sense of being blameworthy, even among those who did not know him. When I try to account for this feeling, I can only guess that it derives from an intuition that Thompson refused to be part of the compromises upon which human survival normally depends. He refused them in order to live in the world of archetypal possibilities out of which all great poetry draws life. A.J.M. Smith, in a dust jacket note for *Stilt Jack*, called it "a world of essences." Many of us feel our lives are only shadows of it, and Thompson's death appeared to cheapen the bargains those who felt blameworthy had made. But I think that at the end Thompson sought, not so much the archetypal world of great poetry, but only silence and peace. In an undated note to a friend, written probably in early 1976, he had said, "the brutal difficulty of life seems to weigh on me heavily. I am developing a profound hatred of my own history and keep asking myself how and why. But it is difficult to think." Like Dylan Thomas and Malcolm Lowry, he found death by water, by a form of drowning, and death by fire, by the spirit of fire. He chose the undifferentiated "limitless ocean," from which everything rises and into which everything falls, of ghazal XXXV. He chose the "cold sea" of ghazal XXX. The last faculty photograph of him published in the Mount Allison yearbook shows an exhausted husk of a man whose eyes seem transfixed by pain and despair. They are the eyes of a man tracked by those Furies evoked in the last line of ghazal XXXVII. Thompson knew he could no longer summon Apollo with arrows of poetry and desire to intercede for him. In ghazal XXX, he had written: "Read it all backwards; start with Act III; / a clean pair of heels." Not for nothing do some lines in the concluding ghazals echo words in *King Lear*. When he wrote them, Thompson was in his own Act V. He knew there was no running left in him. There was only the learning by going away. He chose death, and he had written poems of extraordinary beauty, intensity and breadth of implication and meaning.

Thompson had selected music for his funeral, discussing it with Gibson. He asked for "Guide Me, Oh Thou Great Jehovah" (quoted in ghazal XIV), "Jerusalem," "Abide with Me," "The Day Thou Gavest, Lord, Is Ended" and Cat Stevens's "Morning Has Broken." He is buried in Jolicure Cemetery, a few hundred yards away from the weed-covered site of his house. There is no inscribed marker on his grave. There is only a small boulder, with a curiously swirled, semi-vortical surface. There is also a stubby concrete Royal Canadian Legion cross, and there are occasionally flowers brought there by some of those who knew him and by others who wish they had been among his friends.

A NOTE ON THE TEXT

The texts of the Anansi versions of poems in *At the Edge of the Chopping There Are No Secrets* (1973) and *Stilt Jack* (1978) are not only remarkably free of typographical errors, they adhere closely to Thompson's remaining drafts and typescripts. There are only a few minor differences, too insignificant to note, between versions of poems published in periodicals and their counterparts in the Anansi books. There is a rumour that the published version of *Stilt Jack* differs radically from Thompson's original. I have collated my text of *Stilt Jack* with all published editions and with Thompson's typescript and manuscript versions of individual poems. The few variants recorded in the notes show this rumour to be baseless.

Texts of poems published only in periodicals have been taken as authoritative, and variants from drafts and typescripts have been recorded in the notes.

I have silently corrected minor typographical errors in the translations from René Char; these poems were never published and remain in typescript. Typographical and spelling errors in poems that survive only in draft or typescript form have also been silently corrected. Spelling has not been regularized; it follows the same British or American conventions as the copytexts.

AT THE EDGE OF THE CHOPPING
THERE ARE NO SECRETS

*

STILT JACK

AT THE EDGE OF THE CHOPPING
THERE ARE NO SECRETS

for Meredith

John Thompson at his Wood Point home, about 1968. TIM CRAWFORD

WIFE

Your hands peeling and
    kneading the dough:

the work comes
    up from the thighs

and hips, through
    the leaned shoulders,

sweet drive of arms
    striking

down through the tough roots
    of the fingers;

in the dark
    of the oven

a moon gleams
    and fattens:

our winter bread,

    your shadow
huge on the wall.

bread: a silence; stillness before waking; honeycomb of sleep;
        wood in the heart of its seasoning; the long reach of
        the forest floating away into the half-light; I catch
        your odour out of the eye of my dream;

wine: a green-winged teal fast and sharp under the mist,
        dipping low into the canal; sheaves of early sun on the
        snow, lucent blue in the folds of drifts; tide at the full,
        muddied orange; I go down on my knees before your
        rich bitterness;

salt: a surprising red-hooded bird brings the winter tree
        into being: its shrivelled black apples suddenly
        discover themselves; you have awakened in all your
        bodies, your sharp cry pulls me up into the light.

JOHN THOMPSON

PARTRIDGE

Stopping dead still
    on the road,
a trace of it
    sleeps in the air

(far back in the fir
    a faint rustle)

song:

coiled in spruce bark
an odour:
    buck heat or
the juice of fear;

loving a woman, I know
    death's thicket,

the must of rotting
    crab apples
in an abandoned orchard,

    this partridge
        strutting
through the dying fruit.

OUR ARCS TOUCH

If our arcs touch
it must be

as the taut snow setting
steel; steel
grass blade; death

we won't speak of

our folly,
        so cold, we can

bury these bones:

                        things
rise, the warmth:
so cold

our arcs touch,

it must be.

APPLE TREE

Cauldron of leaves,
the sun a deadly furnace
under the branches;

I cannot contain this summer
nor the charred dancer
exhausted
on the snow:

a head of burnt hair
crackling faintly,
the thin smoke
where a crow drifts
toward no home;

to be possessed or
abandoned by a god
is not in the language,

only the impure, the broken
green, the half-
formed fruit
we reach for in desire,

calling it
our harvest.

HORSE CHESTNUTS

I drive through
   with a clean nail:
      it goes

easy and true through the heart,
   but only with force
      through the tough

undershell, breaking out
   in a jagged, stiff,
      brown flower, crumbs

of yellow flesh spilling;

in the heel of my palm
   the sharp bite
      of the nail-head,

as I thread these fruits on a string
   to hang up in the sun.

JOHN THOMPSON

FISH

a hammer perfectly steel, perfectly
struck

releases it, sweetly, to
rise

live through light water to
strike

what sleeps in a net of steel, blue
sun,

what might have been, wings and sure
release from,

but brings lost taste to metal,
blood,

and a hammer perfectly steel, perfectly
strikes,

what comes to light, live, sun, steel,
deep, from,

stone

HORSE

Your great hooves sunk
   in red mud, massive,
      still, you stare out

over the edge of the world;
   small fires
      flare in your eyes;

the sun turns in hunger
   about your dark head,
      sniffing the earth in you,
tasting your smoke,

and waits for your thighs
   to shift, your hooves
      to strain from the ground,

for some speech from your black muscles:

so the earth would tilt
   under your weight,

hawks plummet upward, the dead
   float in the air like flies,

and we, thrown from our warm furrows,
   relearn our balance,
      reach out in the dark to test

our crooked new bones.

BARN

Lightning struck her
but she didn't burn;
she fed five generations;

the ground's still hers
(they had to tear her down
shingle by shingle)
the green air;

in the muck I'll grow
crazy squash, cucumbers,

dance on my new horizon, watched
by her starry animals.

SCENE

The air warm with filth,
     animal hair, green wood
smoke,

a dimming yellow
     lamp-glow, gathering in

the horizon its
     dainty ships

          gleam of slight
coppery spires,

     a snowy trunk,

this squat boy peeing, quick, back of
     the shed, and

the thock of wood clean-
     split, the blade's
glitter

     just

by the door.

JOHN THOMPSON

BLACK SMITH SHOP

The sun lights blue fires in the black stubble
on this face —
a shapeless rock
my words break on
as his laughter
breaks against the sun;

he has no words but this laughter,
and sounds, loud, crazy,
marrowy sounds which break
chunks out of the light;

but in his shop, in the intense
anthracite light,
not laughter, only

this rhythm of grunts, the face
icy with sweat, moving
with black grace around the horse,

paring crescents of horn from the hooves,
and this moaning speech he must draw,
as he sinks into his labour,

from the flesh of these bodies,
his shining beasts.

Outside again, I break open and shout,
shout,
and my sound comes back to me,

furry, alien, shining,
from the horn of the new moon,
out of this new dark.

At the Edge of the Chopping . . .

TURNIP FIELD

Salt comes in with the wind
off the bay: some days
the air
    is thick with it; it stirs
the roots of the tongue, unearths
and splits the husks of taste —
balsam, marsh-hay, bull-flanks,
    berries, greens

which fuel this green fire,
this burning off
    of the dead hair

of turnips, big as heads,
piled up on the track: meat
for swine and cattle,

plucked junk earth eyes staring
at the man in blue overalls
whose honed fork glitters
in the flame as it
turns the smouldering leaves and stalks,
his mouth full of smoke

so he doesn't taste
fir, grass, muscle, apple,
the wind thick with salt,
but only watches
the way it stirs and
whips up his fires.

AFTER THE RAIN

After the rain, dead
still; not even a crow
menaces;

a hole opens in
the ground of grey cloud:

the wind
must unfold a night
in this hour of dawn.

This is the kind of bird
  will glide into your dreams fluttering
    like a leafy heart —

is this the crow you kept,
  like a weird machine,
    in your refrigerator,

to piece out
  the mechanics of the dark?

CROW AND RABBIT

A crow perching
    on the burst body
of a rabbit,

    shifting
the bones;

itself suddenly
    stilled, aged,
a construction of grey sticks,

giving up dead
    splinter after splinter
to the wind,

but staying as
    the rabbit bones stay,
marking a design on the road.

To lie close, to keep
    hold
of what you have made,
    your own;

cut fir, the green
    gone out of it,
is light, has
the touch of dust on it,

dust the hand taking
    the stain of plant,
weed, soil,
    stays free of in
the work;

a crow's wing nailed
    to the barn side dreams
dark flights,

but the hand keeps, silky,
    to the air,
    sure
of its blood-filled quarrels.

THE IMAGE

A dark flash:
black wings
    on white rock;

now the sun has burned off
    that image
the eye cannot hold;

but the darkness of the bird
still falls,
      swift,
  huge-shadowed

toward eyes holding now
the shining of a river,
      the fatness
of an animal.

FIRST DAY OF WINTER

I step out in the air, it is almost
                blue, the cold
folds around my wrists;

crusty scabs on grey
                maple trunks, the last
faded gold tamarack needles.

JOHN THOMPSON

ZERO

Cold, cold: iron
    blooms on my thighs; I strain
under ground, breaking
    through frozen earth —

then, bang my head,
    viciously, hours,
against the great barn doors, until

fires
crackle in every shingle,

and the huge black roof
    bursts up
a terrified bird,

beats painfully up meadow,
    and crashes

into the frozen hackmatack.

At the Edge of the Chopping . . .

COLD WIND

In this country,
the wind kills
with swift birds
like bronze javelins;

they say, don't
mistake its images,
learn the beat of its cold wings,
the strain of its sinews
gathering on the haft;

and then they tell
of those who got the music
into their marrow:
the old men
who outdid its terror,
beating their tongues like oak leaves
against its fierce metal,

men with the straight eye,
insomniac,
the stubborn song
fast in the bone.

THE GREAT BEAR

You are standing here though you are gone
a thousand miles:

the green world shines, an apple deep
under ice;

I reach out
to stroke the muzzle of the Great Bear, glittering,
dipped, rooting for berries
under the snow in the next meadow.

Your waist is growing lean, your skirt
   slops around your belly:
      you are proud;

you pick over crazy salads and feed me
   salt fish pie
      day after day;

god damn this winter when the air
   and women get thin
      and cold!

Building a fierce fire
   in the furnace, I imagine
      August —

bottles of thick Italian wine,
   huge milky potatoes bursting
      from the moist earth.

JOHN THOMPSON

THE SUPERMARKET INVADED

Lit by the cold
our hungers ride from us,
slovenly beasts,

lope and crackle townwards,
overtaking scared automobiles,
drifting a strange scent
across recoiling thresholds;

inside, they sprawl, gorged,
in apple pulp and the sticky
juice of oranges, sleepily
gnawing marrow bones
and trembling beef hearts;

policemen weep, old ladies
in queer dancing shoes
giggle and shine; children
bang violently on the glass;

while the lord and master of foods,
hysterically red and white,
gobbles bad cheques, bangs
a mad music on the cash register,
and dreams of being easy with women,
learning to drink, and giving
credit unlimited.

At the Edge of the Chopping . . .

DUNG DAY

Flies wake to sip balm, horses
    stare at the new sun;
the dark sinks with the old snow,
and in the alders, partridge bones
    surface;

and you, sluffing through the cold rows,
    pulling young onions;

nothing can be made of time
    or night, but feeling
roots fatten
    in the earth,
smelling moist dung:

a cure for disaster,
white morning
    in this kitchen of dead moons.

JOHN THOMPSON

WHAT ARE YOU ASKING FOR?

What are you asking for?
I give nothing.

Feel, how the light strikes,
    an axe-blade,
across your hand,

and the snow
    cakes on your body:
mud on a sow's belly.

What are you asking for?

You have carried this in your arms
    for hundreds of years,
weightless.

I give nothing.

RETURN

Asleep or on the move where
the land is gone, curved
away, leaving you
blind;

those braille photographs you finger —
the shape: have you
got it?

This is only still
life: close
your ear to the dusty
skin of the city;
listen:

a hunting wing, a form
pressed in the rock,

from the woods where your shadow
glides, the cry
of old blood;

asleep or on the move it's gone
from you with the land curving
down to the cold:

it is time you set out.

JOHN THOMPSON

"WINTER IS BY FAR THE OLDEST SEASON"

— G. Bachelard

Sweet sleep.
I would follow them out of this world
unmarked:

the meadow's snow, undulant,
the woods' cold,

as an animal grazing treads
into the sun and is slowly
burned from the field's edge.

*

With dark comes a fear of horses
and the smell of something moving
in back, always in cover, quick
between the shadows;

the sun is out of reach:
against the light I'd raise
earth, stone.

*

Deer
gone behind days of snow;

through the crook of your arm
I catch the moon
broken with frost;

in shadow
bones persist.

At the Edge of the Chopping . . .

*

Snouts nuzzle the door
night hungry,

quick with our small salt
the table breathes,

we divide cold bread,
sip whiskey chilled in the snow:

the wind a white spice,
cure.

*

Sweet sleep:

the taste of war
and ripeness, smoke
coiling from bones;

to this cold we are
peculiarly knitted:

bitter apples and
crossed blood;

a bucket bangs
on a hackmatack post,

deep below the ice the trout
are perfect.

JOHN THOMPSON

THE SKINS OF A DREAM

Paper birch, way back in the woods,
   whose barks
      curl back like the creamy

skins of a dream, whose whiteness
   curves as the arch
      of this woman's back, swaying,

intent, over the steaming pig's head,
   probing the rind's tenderness
      with a straw,

as the red arc of this windfall apple
   broken by a grey slug sleeping
      in wine, and

way back the woods are wine-dark,
   dark, unfolding
      roots, great stones, bread,

silences,
asking everything.

DOWN BELOW

for Roy Snowdon

At the edge of the chopping there are no secrets:

I am a trout, fat, come out
from under the bank, to lie
in the sun's mouth,
        in mid-stream,

a black fly stilled
        by the quiet, the clean
light, sealed
        in a bead of resin,

a deer's eye resting on white stone;

squatting, at ease with our sweat, smoking,
        there is nothing to say:
one maple shoot, green
        beyond green
is wife to us, we feed
        on roots;

desire and risk sleep, as though
        a candle burned
                far away
by our beds and fires.

JOHN THOMPSON

THE NARROW ROAD

The snowfield rides away and
away, dreaming
of the lips of heaven:
white field bruised with warmth;

geese cry; I wake with them
on the narrow road, dawn
greens new shoots, ice turns milk;

the sweet way riding
beyond this familiar cold sleep.

There is a certain hour to move
without looking (I can almost touch
the end of all trees) to ride
white limits, meet unseen lips:

the great flocks rise to the light.

I like the snow blowing on the floor, things
that enter, rooms where
birds home and sing
as the wind rises, wings
lamping the branches of sleep; I need
no guide but these, and the oil
of woollen socks, and wine;

no goddess whitens my bed;
I am content
to reach into the still cold, without dreams,
listening to the voices fading
on the narrow road.

At the Edge of the Chopping . . .

MOVING OUT, MOVING IN

for R.G.E.

The beauty of dumb animals
long silence
grows on the walls of our house;
the frost imagines our windows;

our water surrounds us with cold voices
of fish and mud;

the woods and
flies, coons, rats draw
our heat into their dark.

*

This is our misfortune
and maybe
our small grace:

we throw words at the dark
and the dark comes
back to us; a bird
is still for a moment
in our garden.

O we are muscular at our
tables, in our beds,
cowards under the moon.

*

JOHN THOMPSON

I know you won't believe this, we are
so obstinate,
don't care for voices,

but after all, the poet names, almost
without speech:

because you are and said so,
we are:

you have opened the windows, the doors,
let in our animals, our sea, our woods;

with you, we inhabit our house,
move out and
let others move in.

BURNT COAT HEAD

We walk without
danger and move

full as the light, a body
without dress, limits,

that sweet
step of the new
foot feeling through
leaf, bark, fibre, and down

now the sap and all green flows
back in sleep, full

light: thus the meadow rises,
greens, dips, shines, steeps from us
into the sea, black;

I know you are here and
speak and the light through you

a meadow, clear green
of light, not calling, the open
shine, sown

with white birds: and above,
above these new birds,

that gathering
of the sun in two eyes
of a cross, killed hawks pointing

JOHN THOMPSON

the meadow falling
to the sea black

the fierce shadows pressing the sun down
rising full, black on this

gallows, two hawks
claiming our day.

PICASSO: *La Jeune Fille sur la Boule*;
LASCAUX: *Stag Frieze*

A pale white horse crops the sky,
    a slender girl
        arms curved up
into the clouds
    stands on the world;

something she does not notice
    is caught
        between her hands,

her body light blue,
    something

caught between her hands:
a child's head, a bowl of apples, a flake
    of the sun,

and the sun through my window tangles
    in the charred antlers
        of five deer
crossing a river under the earth:

the human will not hide its face
    behind the mist.

JOHN THOMPSON

It's in winter I hear you, breathing
  under the snow, weeping
behind a wall of frost.

I don't know whether you are calling me,
  or the team,
long dead, from the barn.

Is it weeping?

On a clean birch hook, the harness
  hangs stiff, so old
the wind can't shift it.

In the half morning, a single gunshot —
  no one hears; the deer
lie warm and still in their yards.

Weeping behind a wall of frost, under the snow
  frozen beets, maybe

your breathing.

I know the brant are wheeling in great flocks in the black rain
over the Jolicure Lakes,
and on the High Marsh Road an old barn, almost the last,
is burning;

I have been watching for hours by the canal, wrists
cold as spent shotgun shells;

water and reeds;

in the last light a new tin barn roof lifts and
cuts like a goose wing: I shoot
and the roof shouts and sinks;

(I have seen men gun so hard their eyes
blacken, their foreheads crack, seamed with frost)

I am half-way back, climbing over a dyke which is
beginning to float:
a man is talking to me in a strange language, or is it
the thin blade of his dyking spade, newly oiled, that speaks?

He is asking why I have murdered and buried his ancestors.

THE CHANGE

It's in the dark we approach
    our energies, that instant
the tide is all fury, still,
    at the full:

as that time I lost an axe-blade
    in the chopping,
and listened, for days, to the rust
    gathering; and that night

I didn't find it, but came upon
    a cow moose blind, stinking
with heat, moaning, and

hooving the black peat with
    such blood, such fury,
the woods broke open, the earth

    recovered her children,
her silences, her poems.

EWE'S SKULL ON THE ABOIDEAU
AT CARTER'S BROOK

Every day I cross the aboideau it's there,
  shifted, less bloody, cleaner, strangely
untouched by dust. As I pass

it seems to rock, gently, in
  a satisfying, crushed sleep, nourishing
the iron blow across the nose.

I wonder why you aren't pure: your pole-axe each time
  in marriage with the bone, your feeding
on blood they, twitching, sleep away;

and the meat, hung, clean from your knife,
  the sweet gods of your barn.

Every day on the aboideau, this ewe's skull,
  bloody, clean:

between these two waters: the salt scummed
  with ice, thick with sea-mud, the fresh,
clear with the iron of the woods,

  under your sign, your bone,
I make my peace.

THE BRIM OF THE WELL

In nests we live on heat,
   small bread, worms:

an arm not lifted against the wind;

    winter on dead twigs, broken grass,
women in small beds, thick
   with cloth, dry;

  rust talk, shrunk fruit;
   seek

   the cold, the wind wrapping
the bone, zero, here

   snow laps the plain, grows
on the spruce wall:
   fruit for children,
for the heart, glittering
   on a stump, a tried blade;

face frost, sniff space, ice,
   for its salt, its soil:

lie with the crow on the dump,
   pass through the wall of his eye:
what brightness of flesh he probes,
   what shadows,
the lip of wound;

whose children are we? We have
   mistaken home.

At the Edge of the Chopping . . .

*

Free of the warmth, outside, something
    happens:
sea hammering softly on a dyke, shingles
    soaked black by rain, smell
of old wood—
    cedar, wings
        beating,
refusing, earth
knowing itself, scenting
    its prey, its grave;

the poem a sheet of blue steel
    hammering
the meadow, fierce

in the air, shreds
    of beaten fruit,
    a bone
from before time, the earth's under
    a curving weave, comb

of a mad cock flaming
    at dawn,
        blood
of a maple split
    by frost,
       lightning, death's
acreage.

*

Not one grain of rust sleeps
on my fury: I insist
    on my wounds, my death:

JOHN THOMPSON
92

clean axe
in new wood

I spring juice.

*

Trees sweet with the bodies
of women clean
to the wind,

green wood burning
to coals, sap hiss.

*

I raise my red arm against the wall of the woods:
salute,
it is eaten
into flashes of snow, catspruce needles, shreds
of faintly flapping birchbark,

a black root full of sound,

coldbroken, earthed, I lie you
lie
would the earth come back to us
not on her breasts
if the earth came back to us
not on her warm belly
when the earth comes back to us
apples black stars broken gardens

on her cold thighs
half buried
in frozen peat.

At the Edge of the Chopping . . .

COMING BACK

Night is day, winter a single
    gust of wind which bangs
        the moon;

the time it takes
    to lift my hand to grasp
        the smell of balsam

I break the buried rock
    of an immense journey

and stand before the window
    my eyes rimy
        with frost, glittering
with owls' flights, my mouth
    full of dead ferns;

around my wife's hand swirls
    a mist of flour,
the hands of my daughter
    gleam with paint,

and I come, simply, bringing
    a few fir cones
which have lain for months
    under the snow,

back to the quiet, knowing
    those terrible iron tongues
no longer hammer
    against the walls of my house.

WAKING

As you wake, watch
    the leaves and branches pull

softly from your flesh and slide
    to the bright window,

your black pig
    and bat shapes

float down into your bones;

raise both your hands
    into the air, and spread

the fingers: see
    how they flutter

from deep within, insanely,
    as the sun strips off

layer after layer of dark feathers,
    the light cutting your body

from the shadows which grow
    from lying down close to yourself.

DAY WITHOUT OMENS

It is that hour when winter, a knife
clean
as the salt wind
probes those wounds we no longer disguise,

lays against the bone its cold voice;

it is a woman suddenly
called back into all her body;

a green branch, this candle,
heedless, still
under our roof;

we resist mystery, the smoke
of old fires:

in the waking of our marrow, now
the call
of this first bird,

the breath of our white voices.

JOHN THOMPSON

THE BREAD HOT FROM THE OVEN

Under the ice with its bouldery death's faces
hidden forms begin to churn the tides,
a wink of blood starts the moon's white track,
fish rise
to their eternal lives;

this morning the bread hot from the oven
sounds with voices:
terrible blows struck
below an unimaginable prairie;

deer break from a mesh of dreams
and two bears burn with the dawn,
cursing the earth's white face
in a stony blood dance
that I feel as words I do not know,
of immense weight,
that I would carry with me,
burdens, until

they appear as they are:
the gods of this place,
this household,
words so light, so still
they are heard only at night
when the earth moves
inwardly:

root songs, that our bodies wake
freighted with melancholy
and the joy of something
a moment held
in our empty hands.

At the Edge of the Chopping . . .

A SLEEPING MAN CURSES THE SUMMER

Without darkness, with no
edge of things,

the sun whitening in an endless
green field,

udders huge — the fat
of all: sown
to sleep,

the orchard lunatic with apples.

Would the fox come
    from the drowse, the deer
quickening
quiver into the plains,

a flicker of night at midday,
    the silent frost
thinning the stars,

and the green withered
    to a dark edge, beyond which

the black: your real
    hands and eyes.

THE ONION

I have risen from your body
full of smoke, charred fibres;

the light kicks up off
the glazed snow: I have to
turn from its keenness,
its warmth, seeking
darkness, burying ground;

I am without grace, I cannot shape
those languages, the knots
of light and silence:
the newness of being
still, the press
of the snow's whiteness.

Young steers turned from the barn
stand, furry stones, streaked
with dung,
cold light, thin
February snow.

In this kitchen warmth I reach
for the bouquet
of thyme and sage, drifting
in the heat: a world crumbles
over my hands, I am washed
with essences;

At the Edge of the Chopping . . .

I cup the onion I watched grow all summer:
cutting perfectly through its heart
it speaks a white core, pale
green underskin, the perfections
I have broken, that curing grace
my knife releases;

and then you are by me, unfolded
to a white stillness, remade warmth on warmth.

So we turn from our darkness,
our brokenness,
share this discovered root,
this one quiet bread
quick with light, thyme, that deep
speech of your hands which always
defeats me, calling me through strange earths
to this place suddenly yours.

STILT JACK

for my daughter,
and for S.

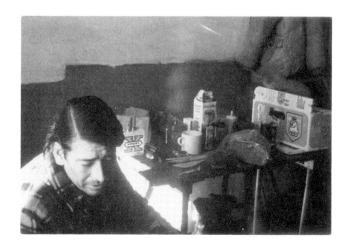

John Thompson at Jolicure, winter, 1974. Coll. SHIRLEY MANN GIBSON

Those great sea-horses bare their teeth and laugh at the dawn.
W. B. YEATS

May God preserve the sickness of my eye.
TRUMBULL STICKNEY

I have only to lift my eyes, to see the Heights of Abraham.

Originating in Persia, the ghazal is the most popular of all the classical forms of Urdu poetry. Although the form as it is now written first appeared in Persia, it probably goes back to the 9th century. The great master of the ghazal in Persia was Hafiz (1320-1389). Five hundred years later, Ghalib, writing in Urdu, became an equally brilliant master of the form, which is full of conventions, required images, and predetermined postures.

The ghazal proceeds by couplets which (and here, perhaps, is the great interest in the form for Western writers) have no necessary logical, progressive, narrative, thematic (or whatever) connection. The ghazal is immediately distinguishable from the classical, architectural, rhetorically and logically shaped English sonnet.

The link between couplets (five to a poem) is a matter of tone, nuance: the poem has no palpable intention upon us. It breaks, has to be listened to as a song: its order is clandestine.

The ghazal has been practised in America (divested of formal and conventional obligations) by a number of poets, such as Adrienne Rich. My own interest in the "form" lies in the freedom it allows — the escape, even, from brief lyric "unity." These are not, I think, surrealist, free-association poems. They are poems of careful construction; but of a construction permitting the greatest controlled imaginative progression.

There is, it seems to me, in the ghazal, something of the essence of poetry: not the relinquishing of the rational, not the abuse of order, not the destruction of form, not the praise of the private hallucination.

The ghazal allows the imagination to move by its own nature: discovering an alien design, illogical and without sense — a chart of the disorderly, against false reason and the tacking together of poor narratives. It is the poem of contrasts, dreams, astonishing leaps. The ghazal has been called "drunken and amatory" and I think it is.

John Thompson

I
———————————————————————————

Now you have burned your books: you'll go
with nothing but your blind, stupefied heart.

On the hook, big trout lie like stone:
terror, and they fiercely whip their heads, unmoved.

Kitchens, women and fire: can you
do without these, your blood in your mouth?

Rough wool, oil-tanned leather, prime northern goose down,
a hard, hard eye.

Think of your house: as you speak, it falls,
fond, foolish man. And your wife.

They call it the thing of things, essence
of essences: great northern snowy owl; whiteness.

II

In this place we might be happy; blue-
winged teal, blacks, bats, steam

from cows dreaming in frost.
Love, you ask too many questions.

Let's agree: we are whole: the house
rises: we fight; this is love

and old acquaintance.
Let's gather the stars; our fire

will contain us; two,
one.

III

It's late. Tu Fu can't help me. There's no wind.
My blue shirt hangs from the cuffs on the line.

I can't talk to God. Tonight, I dug
three hills of potatoes. Sadness, what's that?

Give up words: a good knife, honed; and a needle
drawn across an iron bar, set in a matchbox.

Damn these men who would do my work for me;
my tomatoes redden by the window.

All spring and summer (this inch,
these noosed three moons) I fished trout.

One line of poetry dogs me; the newspapers,
the crazy world.

I'm thinking of you. Nashe. Rats on my window sill.
The dirt under my fingernails.

Lord, lord. I'm thinking of you.
I'm gone.

IV

I fed my marrow with the juices of clams,
oysters, raw onions, moose heart and black olives:

a green crust, a man banging a raw
elbow-bone on my table, stopped me.

I thought all women were beautiful, and I was ready:
drunk, I'd lie with dark iron; sober, walk away.

There's a health will lead me to the grave, the worm;
resisting axioms, I'll dream,

lie down on my right side, left side, eat dung:
Isaiah greets me; he wants to talk; we'll feed.

V

Don't talk to me of trifles; I feel the dirt in these:
what brightens when the eye falls, goes cold.

I have so many empty beer bottles, I'll be rich:
I don't know what I'd rather be: the Great Bear, or stone.

I feel you rocking in the dark, dreaming also
of branches, birds, fire and green wood.

Sudden rain is sweet and cold. What darkens
those winds we don't understand?

Let's leave the earth to be; I'm asleep.
The slow sky shuts. Heaven goes on without us.

VI
_____

My daydreams defeat me, and cigarettes;
in the cold I'm myself: two follies.

I want to cut myself off. Bone says:
I'll dance, and you with me.

Bats flit at close of eve; anger
dies with the wind; partridge roost.

The moon, the moon, the moon.
A pine box; Herodotus; no tears, a settling:

what lies in its right place, lives. Brothers,
sisters, true friends lie down in darkness.

Dreams and the cold: I'm drunk on these.
Sisters, brothers, fathers, friends, I don't forget.

VII

Terror, disaster, come to me from America.
Middle of the night. Highs in the seventies. Penny Lane. Albany.
                                        Albany?

What letters of van Gogh I remember, I've forgotten.
He cut off his ear. Crows. Potato eaters.

Crazy squash, burnt tomatoes, char of poems, sour milk,
a candle gone down: is this my table?

I'm waiting for Janis Joplin: why,
why is it so dark?

I talk to a poet: he goes on, drunk:
I pray he's writing, don't dare ask.

Hang on, hang on: I'm listening,
I'm listening to myself.

VIII

I forget: why are there broken birds
behind me; words, goddammit, words.

I want to wake up with God's shadow
across me: I'm a poet, not a fool.

Porcupine are slow, fast in their quills:
they'll come to your iron bar, believing themselves and apples.

I don't want to die bloody on the highway:
I travel back roads, the dirt;

don't complain about going: sometimes
think I'll never get to sleep.

Everything reminds me. I want to push.
Black spruce; strange fires.

Snow will come. Wind. A kind of age.
What's at my feet must move quickly.

October; 3 a.m.; I go out and take a rose,
and the sea, and thorns.

I want to give everything to this burnt flower: I've nothing;
I bury my face; set it in water.

IX

Yeats. Yeats. Yeats. Yeats. Yeats. Yeats. Yeats.
Why wouldn't the man shut up?

The word works me like a spike harrow:
by number nine maybe I get the point.

It's all in books, save the best part; God knows
where that is: I found it once, wasn't looking.

I've written all the poems already,
why should I write this one:

I'll read Keats and eye the weather too,
smoke cigarettes, watch Captain Kangaroo.

Big stones, men's hands, the shovel
pitched properly. The wall of walls rises.

If I weren't gone already, I'd lie down right now:
have you ever heard children's voices?

Sometimes I think the stars scrape at my door, wanting in:
I'm watching the hockey game.

Likely there's an answer: I'm waiting,
watching the stones.

X
_____

A pineapple tree has grown in this kitchen
two years, on well water. Right here,

a man went to set a fire in the stove
and the blaze froze on the match.

Those winds: in summer turn the head rancid, in winter
drive a cold nail through the heart down to the hardwood floor.

Daisies, paintbrush, bellflower, mustard, swamp iris;
hackmatack, crowns driven northeast: they're there.

Pigs fattened on boiled potatoes; horses mooning in hay;
in the woodshed he blew his head off with a shotgun.

XI

The fox is quick; I haven't seen him; he's quick.
the rainbow strikes one foot at my door.

The kettle lid lifts: must be fire,
it keeps.

It's too dry to plough; gulls grow in the cut corn,
owls, harriers: so many swift wings.

There's all the noise here,
it's so quiet:

the sky sleeps on the backs of cattle,
streams slow to black.

Last night I died: a tired flie woke me.
On White Salt Mountain I heard a phrase carving the world.

XII

after Tu Fu

I'm here at last, love this bed:
we stay up at night talking the moon down.

A bad mistake: looking for new flowers,
finding frost.

We'll fish tommy cod: that's enough;
come April I know where to go.

If the man gives me enough pennies
I'll go across the marsh and buy a little field.

Why be my own Job's comforter?
A bottle of cheap rye: an empty head.

JOHN THOMPSON

XIII

The rook-delighting heaven?
I've seen one crow.

The cock pheasant I'll nail: he's beautiful,
quick; I know the tree, the spot; He's disappeared.

They dragged him home behind the tractor:
fat beef; the dark wound in the loam.

I think we should step out the door:
they're calling: men, women and dead voles.

I wish there were less wine: I'd want more;
breasts, breasts.

I'm in touch with the gods I've invented:
Lord, save me from them.

XIV

All night the moon is a lamp on a post;
things move from hooks to beautiful bodies. Drunk.

I think I hear the sound of my own grief:
I'm wrong: just someone playing a piano; just.

Bread of heaven.
                    In close.

In dark rooms I lose the sun:
what do I find?

Poetry: desire that remains desire. Love?
The poet: a cinder never quite burned out.

XV

If I give everything away
it's because I want to take everything;

catching things from the air, I'll force
a perfect flower from the blue snow;

I can look at the sun with open eyes,
the moon laughs in my kitchen;

I think of children and the unwise:
they have terrible strength;

when will you,
will you?

The drunk and the crazy live for ever,
lovers die:

our mouths are wet with blood:
is it the blood we'll live by?

If I give you my right arm,
will you

XVI

The barn roof bangs a tin wing in the wind;
I'm quite mad: never see the sun;

you like sad, sad songs that tell a story;
how far down on whiskey row am I?

I believe in unspoken words, unseen gods:
where will I prove those?

If I wash my hands will I disappear?
I'll suck oil from Tobin's steel and walnut.

If one more damn fool talks to me about
sweetness and light . . .

I'm looking for the darkest place;
then, only then, I'll raise my arm;

someone must have really socked it to you:
were the lips made to hold a pen or a kiss?

If there were enough women I wouldn't write poetry;
if there were enough poetry

XVII

I pick things out of the air: why not?
No one shall sleep.

Lift me up, lift me up . . . , he said:
I would have, I would.

I don't need Page's arm:
I've got fire: I'm laughing, laughing.

We've all been cold. I was born mad.
Wooden matches strike anywhere.

If there's joy for one day, there is, there is:
they that sow in teares: shall reap in joy.

Celebrate. Celebrate. Celebrate.
Death cannot celebrate thee.

One fish, one bird,
one woman, one word,

that does it for me, and the last word of *Ulysses* is
yes.

XVIII

A man dancing into life:
ashes to ashes; O my America.

Friends, I believe I'll burn first:
I'll find you by compass: dead reckoning.

Sing no sad songs. A tree stands:
lay a stone against it.

Cast a cold eye, cast
a cold eye:

when I meet you again I'll be all light,
all dark, all dark.

JOHN THOMPSON
124

XIX

I try for oblivion, dirt
and a woman:

my right hand breaks;
new snow;

I drive into a strange heart, and lift
out of all this beauty something

myself, a fish hook tinged with blood,
a turned furrow,

potatoes, fish, those who love them,
must come.

XX

I begin again:
why should not young men be mad?

Trial of my own images, I dream
of one thing.

The curve of a line weaves
a celestial equator:

My child. The dark
horse in the rain.

Let Meton speak, but leave
the numbers lie as stones.

I pick over
last night's food.

Now let us servants rise like Atlantis.
By lying down, I'll wake, depart in peace.

The tide ebbs from my hand.
I want to join blood.

Loaves of bread remembered:
eat salt and tell the truth.

Grief the knife, joy
the vulnerable bread.

Eat, let the blade
be surprised by joy.

XXI

I know how small a poem can be:
the point on a fish hook;

women have one word or too many:
I watch the wind;

I'd like a kestrel's eye and know
how to hang on one thread of sky;

the sun burns up my book:
it must be all lies;

I'd rather be quiet, let the sun
and the animals do their work:

I might watch, might turn my back,
be a done beer can shining stupidly.

Let it be: the honed barb drowsing in iron water
will raise the great fish I'll ride

(dream upon dream, still the sun warms my ink
and the flies buzzing to life in my window)

to that heaven (absurd) sharp fish hook,
small poem, small offering.

XXII

I'm just a man who goes fishing:
if there's a woman with green eyes, there is.

My land's wet: I'll wait, perched on a post;
I know my seed will alarm the sun.

Dark April, black water, cold wind,
cold blood on a hook.

I won't scream when I die:
I've burned everything;

words swarm on the back of my hand.
I don't run,

thick with honey
and sweet death

I love to watch the trout rising
as I fall, fall.

XXIII

What is it you want to say? Say it now.
I hear children; the fallow; pig's blood.

Churn, churn; all in black:
the milk I want, I want.

There must be an end:
flowers deceive me;

we are all poor, poor:
the cattle lift their huge eyes.

Where am I? Where are you?
The Lord stuck on a bulletin board.

Put two words together: likely
it's your name.

I don't know mine:
the words have taken it, or someone's hand.

I dream myself into being,
a poor man.

I'm a great fish, swallowing everything:
drunk all my own seas.

Say it now: honey from the sweet, drunk, dead:
I lift my eyes,

I'm listening; the moon sinks;
I chart the back of my hand.

I don't hear your words: I hear the wind,
my dreams, disasters, my own strange name.

Always the light: a strange moon,
and the green I don't understand;

knives set in order; somewhere else,
eyes looking back across a terrible space:

a meeting in a garden, hands, knees, feet
in the dirt: animals; the flies feeding;

what comes from this? pour wine on it:
have you read all your blood?

No prophecy in the furrow: only the print of bare feet,
anxious for what grows;

nothing? one small leaf is a heart:
a leaf we divide, dividing us.

Lift up the soily stones,
feel the burn of lime,

a handful of seeds, a handful of earth,
silence in thunder on the tongue:

a long waiting without stars,
ending in snow.

XXV

In a dark wood,
and you in a strange bed.

In midsummer I dream great snows
and a man come to ask about fish.

Divinity sounds in machines,
shines darkly from the pleasure of birds.

What do I believe? I hear the crack
of corn fattening at night.

The blood at night sounds
with your swimming.

Where are all our books and stories?
I look into dark water:

We have been there: our eyes
join deep below the surface.

If I ask questions, you'll show me
some beautiful thing you have made.

XXVI

Surrounded by dirty glasses, nights
of love: the world is full of . . .

and then to be honest, as a hair,
a still hand, a plain box;

caught by bad music, strange meat,
the smell of old tin;

there are ways, and signs: the woods
point one way.

the words: there is a word:
there are words, lie about us,

dogs and the night and children
poured out in looseness

and children
on the grassy ground.

JOHN THOMPSON

XXVII

You have forgotten your garden (she said)
how can you write poems?

That things go round and again go round.
In the middle of the journey . . .

Folly:
the wildflowers grow anyway.

I wait for a word, or the moon, or whatever,
an onion, a rhythm.

All the rivers look for me,
find me, find me.

The small stone in my hand weighs years:
it is dark.

To turn, and remember, that
is the fruit.

XXVIII

I learn by going;
there is a garden.

Things I root up from the dirt
I'm in love with.

First things: lost. The milky saucer,
of last things a siren.

Please, please be straight, strait,
stone, arrow, north needle.

I haven't got time for the pain,
name your name,

the white whale, STILT JACK, in her face,
where I have to go.

XXIX

The Lord giveth.
I wrote letters,

sealing,
stitches of emptiness.

Absence makes what?
Presence, presence.

Music, beautiful stories,
tin, tin cans,

fingers on a pine table,
fire.

Love, black horse, a turned
head, voice:

breaking my heart, laughing;
knife, fork and spoon,

turnips, stored words, rip-rap and all that
etcetera,

something
taken away.

XXX

The mind tethered, head
banged with a hardwood stick;

sense a mangled iron
and the fire gone cold.

Read it all backwards; start with Act III;
a clean pair of heels.

The muck of endings; drunk beginnings;
yattering histories, rodomontades, anabases.

Get to the bloody point:
seize the needle,

day, plainness: cold sea, that
one grain of sand.

XXXI

I'll wait; watch
Look, look.

Poor people. Poor
We're rich; beautiful.

Brant: the Great Missaquash Bog:
My love: a splash: safe.

I fire my right arm out strait.
My wife's sledgehammer; my woman's eye.

I'm not good enough.
Sufficient is Thine arm alone.

XXXII

A woman to quench the fires of my eye:
song: sweet, comely song.

We sing hymns: we care
for the sound of grief and the grieving.

But we'll dance, her ashen hair
tenting my body;

we join hands, eyes, lips: one:
as safe as a toad in God's pocket.

Love the final loss, the last
giving.

This is the day which the Lord hath made;
we will rejoice and be glad in it.

XXXIII

Dark as the grave. The deep lightning
whiteness of swans' wings.

I make necklaces for a woman and
my daughter: gentle harvests.

Anger dies with the wind. In near-sleep
I'm a salt-water trout spilling seed.

The want. The hunting harrier
bound to earth. The fox denned.

I go clothed like a bear: ride
against the sun. Then the snow sleep:

I have only to lift my eyes to see
the Heights of Abraham.

XXXIV

I surrender to poetry, sleep
with the cinders of Apollo.

Belay to words:
Stubai, Kernmantel, Bonnaiti,

Karrimor, K2, Nanga Parbat,
Jumar, Eiger, Chouinard, Vasque.

Annapurna. The mountain wakens:
a closing hand.

Love lies with snow, passion
in the blue crevasse. Grief on summits.

Let me climb: I don't know to what:
north face, south face?

Maybe the roping down,
the last abseil.

XXXV

after Mir Taqi Mir

Love, look at my wounds, the shame I've drunk —
I wouldn't wish such suffering on my bitterest enemy.

Walk the graveyards: did you know the dead could have such hair?
But devouring fate would have gnawed at them forever.

You're well off: don't make your home with this history of
disasters:
The cold desert always destroys my bed.

I know: your pale green eyes speak what's final:
Sweet deaths never spoken of, beautiful terrors.

It's clear: the broken moon is suddenly full for me.
As always, drops gather into a limitless ocean.

XXXVI

I don't know

Desire.
Taste of the sea: salt.

The scorch of letters written
from the poem's isolate place.

I feel all the weight:
have I dared the dark centre?

We'll rise as one body.
A wedge of geese.

Time: slow as rivers,
entering us as the wings of birds.

Soft now. The join deep as bone.
Safe as the unwounded sap.

When you look into my eyes,
The moon stills as a Kestrel.

We'll gather all our lives and deaths
In a lightning harvest.

XXXVII

Now you have burned your books, you'll go with nothing.
A heart.

The world is full of the grandeur,
and it is.

Perfection of tables: crooked grains;
and all this talk: this folly of tongues.

Too many stories: yes, and
high talk: the exact curve of the thing.

Sweetness and lies: the hook, grey deadly bait,
a wind and water to kill cedar, idle men, the innocent

not love, and hard eyes
over the cold,

not love (eyes, hands, hands, arm)
given, taken, to the marrow;

(the grand joke: *le mot juste:*
forget it; remember):

Waking is all: readiness:
you are watching;

I'll learn by going:
Sleave-silk flies; the kindly ones.

XXXVIII

Should it be passion or grief?
What do I know?

My friend gives me heat and a crazy mind.
I like those (and him).

Will it all come back to me?
Or just leave.

I swing a silver cross and a bear's tooth
in the wind (other friends, lovers, grieving and passionate).

I've looked long at shingles:
they've told.

I'm still here like the sky
and the stove.

Can't believe it, knowing nothing.
Friends: these words for you.

JOHN THOMPSON

PART II: Uncollected Poems and Translations

EARLY UNCOLLECTED
POEMS AND TRANSLATIONS

[LA CLOCHE QUI SONNE]

La cloche qui sonne
Ses moments
Mourants
M'attrape, sur un point
Éternel
Des mondes qui n'ont jamais existé;
Je me sens
Qui brûle
Dans les feux
Les yeux
Impénétrables
De la mort.

THE DEAD LOST ON THE EIGER

The glass gales fling a winter
Of claws scythe-whirling, bitter
Into the humped bone
Back of the crouched ice-man
Who hangs by the threads of fire
Of his soul,
At the crux of death
On the swallowing wall;

On a distant balcony, an old
Man's eye is fixed
To the axe-flash moment's stillness
And the drumming line.

*

I am the roots of my own tree
My own dead branch I fling;
I am my own enemy
My own defeats I sing;
I am the tides in my own sea
My own seventh bell I ring.

But by my body she fought in
My lips in hers rejoice:
My arching trunk is by her whim
My life is by her choice;

And now she is my own stripped limb
Whose stump shouts with her voice.

JOHN THOMPSON

*

Say, then, what you saw there
Softly through salt lips,
There where sunlight struck a name
Across a cracked and root clenched face;
Tell how the late horizon cast
Its silence, quivering
Across the flickered liquid glass
The wind-turned touch on sand
Sun-flecked flesh;
And would that be enough?
No, let your eye
In salt silence like the sea recall
The solitary, dark cry
Of a white bird hung between
Time and time
Over the water's waiting throat.

THE DRUNKEN BOAT

after Arthur Rimbaud

As I went down the unheeding rivers,
I felt no longer guided by the haulers:
Screaming Redskins had taken them for targets,
Nailing them naked to stakes of colours.

I spared no thought for the crew,
Carrier of Flemish grain and English cottons.
When these uproars disappeared with my haulers,
The currents let me go down where I wished.

In the furious clashing tides,
The other winter, more mute than infants' brains,
I ran! And the cast-off peninsulas
Did not endure more triumphant confusions.

The tempest blessed my sea awakenings.
Lighter than a cork I danced the waves
Which are called the eternal victim-rollers,
Ten nights, without regretting the stupid beacon's eye!

Sweeter than the flesh of sour apples to children
The green waters seeped into my pine hulk,
Cleansing me of vomit and blue wine stains
And scattering rudder and anchor.

And from then, I bathed myself in the Poem
Of the Sea, milky and star-infused,
Devouring the green azures; where, enraptured, pale
Flotsam — the drowned dead — sometimes sink down;

Where, suddenly staining the blueness, frenzies
and slow rhythms under the day's crimson fire,
Stronger than alcohol, vaster than our lyres
The bitter blood-red stains of love ferment!

I know the lightning-burst sky, and the waterspouts,
The surfs and currents; I know the evening,
The dawn exalted like a multitude of doves,
and I have seen sometimes what man believed he saw.

I have seen the sunken sun, mystic horror-stained,
Illuminating with vast violet clots,
Like actors of very ancient dramas,
The shuttered shimmering of distant rolling waves.

I have dreamed the green night of glittering snows,
The slow kiss climbing to the sea's eyes,
The circulation of extraordinary saps,
The yellow and blue awakening of the phosphorus singers!

I have followed, for full months, like manic herds,
The swell's assault upon the reefs
Not thinking that the Marys' luminous feet
Could muzzle the panting Oceans!

Know you that I smashed into unbelievable jungles
Mingling with flowers the eyes of man-skinned panthers
Rainbows stretched like bridles
Under the horizon of the seas, to sea-green herds.

I saw enormous morasses ferment, weirs
Where a Leviathan rots in the weeds!
Water-chaoses in the middle of calm seas
and the distance cataracting into chasms!

Glaciers, silver suns, pearled waves, smouldered-coal skies,
Hideous wrecked ships in the depths of dark gulfs
Where giant serpents devoured by insects
Drop from twisted trees, with black perfumes!

I would have loved to show to children these dolphins
Of the blue wave, these golden, these singing fish.
Flower-flecked surfs lulled my drift
At moments winged by ineffable winds.

From time to time, wearied martyr of the poles and zones,
The sea whose sobs gentled my rolling
Pushed up to me its yellow-vesseled flowers of shadows
And I remained like a woman on her knees! . . .

Almost isle, tossing on my shores the quarrels
And the droppings of clamorous blond-eyed birds.
And I sailed on, when across my frail cords
The falling drowned ones sank to their sleep! . . .

Then I, boat lost under the hairs of coves,
Tempest-hurled into the birdless ether,
I, whose sea-drunk carcass the Monitors
And Hanseatic sailboats would not have fished out;

Free, smoking, scaly with violet mists,
I who pierced the smouldering wall of the sky
Who carry exquisite potents to the good poets,
Lichens of the sun and mucus of the azur;

Who ran branded with electric crescent moons
Mad ship escorted by black sea-horses
When the Julys brought down with bludgeon strokes
The ultramarine skies to ardent waterspouts;

I who trembled, feeling from fifty leagues the moan
Of rutting Behemoths and dense Maelstroms,
Eternal weaver of the blue immobilities,
I regret ancient-parapeted Europe!

I have seen starred archipelagos and islands
Whose fevered skies are open to the voyager,
Is it in these bottomless nights that you sleep and exile yourself
A million golden birds, O future Vigour?

But truly I have wept too much! The dawns are harrowing
Each moon is atrocious and all suns bitter:
Acrid love swells me with intoxicating torpors.
O may my boat smash! Let me go to the sea!

If I desire a water of Europe, it is the puddle
Black and cold, where toward the embalmed twilight
A squatting child, sadness-filled, launches
A boat frail as a butterfly of May.

Bathed in your langour, O waves, I can no longer
Cross the wakes of cotton-carrying ships,
Nor pass the proud display of flags and pennants,
Nor float under the horrible eyes of prison-hulks.

THE MAN IN THE WIND

an elegy for Dylan Thomas

Though they be mad and dead as nails,
Heads of the characters hammer through daisies;
Break in the sun till the sun breaks down
And death shall have no dominion — Dylan Thomas

By the druid-circled hill
Shadowed . . . sea fisted shore,
With gull scream and white
Wave claws' rage he came
To begin his ruining voyage;
Gathered the soils, the waters
And the sounding sky until
They smouldered in his tongue's blood.

Thirty-nine years, mad
In one eye and in the other
Drunk, climbing the sky,
With a raw fist scattering
The naked furnace flames
To snatch his words
And set the night on fire,
To mark his way to death
Across the dark tracked
And syllabled altar-fields.

He, in the black sun-storm
Chaosed abyss, reviver of
A savage French boy's mystic words,

Framed from the terrible action
Of the smouldering ice-brain
Another Eden's surgery,
Fashioned a blood-struck grief
Of seasons, until the locks

Of the world broke down and died;
And who can know
The sulphur blood which drove
The darkness of his pen,
The nails which hung him
Hammered to a cross of words,
The torn and torrent light which caught
The deep lost tears of innocence.

And for the fools who saw
That he could laugh, but not
The irony, he played the fool,
And though they may have sensed
His singing war of love
They saw not the terror sheet,
The black sail of his grave.

And now, under a tall hill of Wales
He lies who dared
To feed the fury of his own dark fire.
And yet I see, under the wind-weather breaking sky,
The shroud-stone druid heron stands, and celebrates
The earth's first final praising blood.

A TALE OF THE MOON

The sea was the singer
And I the lunar man
Circling the sky-engraving masts
The voice-distance drifting sails
Cast on the watching dark ship-eyes
My symphony light white-
Flowered wash of snow;

And from the green black-deep
Whirl-tided fathom graves
Called out the ancient raw eye-scarred
Thick root-hung cracked stone age-faced
Midnight player of the spun gold
Whisper-thread strung wave harp
To jewel the sea's song;

Then sea-chant and crystal
Frail finger trembled harp
Fashioned the fabled music-sphere
The glass heaven sounding cage
Which held the first-formed woman shape
Come blood-incandescent
Pure Eden's enchantress

Who sang to the tall ships
And ocean water chords,
To the stone-staring prophet eyes,
Sang with a night-rending voice
Which forced light to the black sea-face
And turned the stars to tears:
It is the time to tell,

JOHN THOMPSON

The time to break the night
Horizon's prison line,
To summon the sun-kingdom light
And set the toiled sea on fire;
And the sea and the ancient man
Knew death in their dark song,
And wind drummed to the sails;

And I, moon-man, saw this:
The shattered spun-glass cage
Splinter-flame cast the watching flesh
Of man sea and ships to fire
And woman-shape turn to burning
Blood-furnace climbing sphere
The sun-poem of the dawn.

A FEVER ON THE RIVER

There is a fever on the river,
White petals and twigs, swollen
Limbs of dolls, discarded bread,
Slow blisters of yellow rain;
The last music gone from the bridges;
Two torn shoes dangling from the wharf,
Muck-scaled scuffed hide eyes staring;
What do feet know but hard stone and dirt?

The fisherman's line is limp,
His eyes full of dark breasts,
Trembling since sunset burned
Down the buildings on the further shore;
Lips nibbling in the flesh;
His concern is not with silence,
He knows the terror of drowning;
Winds in the stained empty hook
Shuffles toward wine and nakedness;
Silence of the waters' syllables,
Waters which once bred fish;
There is a fever on the river.

The river has never loitered,
Its blood is a multitude
Of voices, ice caught in sleep,
A day's field of flowers, cut
At the throat, love-lies-bleeding,
The arrogant thighs of hills,
The chaste tree taken before dawn,
Birds, majestic birds, who thought
The season ripe to fish;

Voices which have said the world
In silence to the summer,
In anger to tall proud houses
And the pale bones of men;
Their concern was not with silence;
The river has never loitered.

Only the sea can receive lost words;
The darkness must decay to salt,
The river has no love, and need
Not turn around, it is violent,
And has the fertility of violence,
Its tongue knows the bitterness
Of tongues that are not heard;
Only the sea can receive lost words.

INCANTATION FOR A NEW SEASON

I

Winter of rag sparrows and old green bread,
Magicians and burning worlds
Dumped out with the Christmas tree.

In broad night, with no cunning, a black frost
Throttled the orange and bit out
The eyes of a young woman.

A dry butterfly dissolved under a pin;
A young girl slashed off her long locks
For the New Year, out of spite.

II

We recall that the summer took place
In the middle of a bright field, and was
A fat bee splashing in a blue flower;

That the summer was a young girl with
A nose hot with smells: dark fruit and dense
Perfumes, the blood of white horses;

That the summer trees drifted out of sight
Into the darkening horizon, and rose
Sun-clothed spiralling birds in white flight.

JOHN THOMPSON

III

We clutch for a new season, a new
Dreaming of the frozen eye: the sharp
Gemstone of dark ice a moment from
A new sun's blitz; the blue deep
Delicate explosion of the Spring's flower.

VENUS ANADYOMENE

—Arthur Rimbaud

As from a coffin of green zinc, the greased
Brown hair of a woman's head arises
From an old bathtub, stupid like a beast,
The bald spots patched with ill contrived disguises;

Then the fat grey neck, the shoulder blades that
Jut out huge; then the short back knobbed and troughed;
The plump buttocks seem to balloon aloft;
Beneath the skin long slabs of blubbery fat;

The spine's quite red; and the whole thing promotes
A strangely horrifying stench; one notes
Peculiar spots for study with a lens;

Engraved words — Clara Venus — the buttocks bear;
— The whole body shifts, the huge rump extends
The hideous beauty of an anal ulcer.

POEM ON TWO PAINTINGS OF VAN GOGH

The Painter on the Road to Tarascon and *Wheat Fields with Crows.*

In the shattered fire of the dawn
The charred blue noon
Already whispers;
Dark gods point
From the awakening cobblestones
And the still white palm of the corn;
Unknown birds rustle in the palette.

The flesh is cast down on the road,
A black shadow,
But sailing, blacker
And more swift than the sun;
The pack is full of stars.

The sun knows but cannot
Escape the blue stride full of eyes,
Voracious, intent
On their starry burden,
Their bright death.

The day blooms into storm;
The skies give up their dead
From flashing shreds of shroud;
The earth in fear unleashes
Its atrocious abundance:

The fruit is a glittering beak,
The corn a clamor of wings —
Dark harvest!
Through the blue distances,

Over the drunken fields,
Sail the sun-devouring birds:
The hand becomes a twisted cypress leaf,
The heart in mid-stride
Welcomes the gentle claw.

TRANSLATIONS FROM RENÉ CHAR

John Thompson at Wood Point, about 1968. TIM CRAWFORD

ROUGEUR DES MATINAUX

(Delible Enclave)

to Henry Mathieu

The facts and their approximations are collective. Truth is individual.

Take care: not everyone is worthy of trust.

The accolade to him who, emerging from his fatigue and sweat, will approach and say to me, "I have come to deceive you."

O great black barrier, on the way to your death, why should it always be you who points out the lightning flash?

I

The rising sun's state of mind is lively joy despite the cruel day and its remembrance of the night. The bloodstain becomes the crimson of dawn.

II

When your mission is to awaken, you begin by washing in the river. Both the first delight and the first shock are for you.

III

Press your luck, embrace your happiness and go toward your risk. They will grow accustomed to watching you.

IV

When the storm rages at its height, there is always a bird to hearten us. An unknown bird. It sings before flying away.

Translations from René Char

V

Wisdom does not mean massing together, but, through creation and the common spirit, finding our number, our mutual agreements, our differences, our way through, our truth and that ounce of despair which is its goad and its swirling mist.

VI

Head for the essential: don't you need young trees to restock your forest?

VII

Intensity is silent and still. Its image is not. (I love what dazzles me and then accentuates the darkness deep within me.)

VIII

How much this world suffers, to become man's world, to be built within the four walls of a book! That it should, consequently, be put back into the hands of fools and speculators who force it to progress faster than its natural pace, how can we not see in this something more than ill luck? To combat this calamity, whatever the cost, with the aid of its own magic, to open in the wing of the path, from what is there, insatiable excursions — that is the task of the Matinaux. Death is only a profound and pure sleep with the plus sign which pilots it and helps it cleave the wave of becoming. Why be alarmed by your alluvial state? Stop taking the branch for the trunk and the root for the void. It's a small beginning.

IX

One must blow on several weak flames to make a good blaze. Beautiful burned eyes bring the gift to perfection.

JOHN THOMPSON
170

X

Formidable female, she carries rage in her bite and a mortal cold in her flanks, this knowledge which, part of a noble ambition, ends by finding its measure in our tears and our strangulation. Do not misjudge, O you among the best whose arm she covets and over whose failings she keeps watch.

XI

What owes nothing to man, but wishes us well, exhorts, with every pressure to break with our luck, our morale, and to submit to some simplifying model: "Rebel, rebel, rebel . . ."

XII

The individual adventure, the prodigal adventure, community of our dawns.

XIII

Conquest and indefinite conservation of this conquest *ahead of us* who whisper our shipwreck and throw our deception off course.

XIV

Sometimes we have this peculiarity of swaying as we walk. The times feel light to us, the ground smooth, our feet turn only deliberately.

XV

When we say: *the heart* (and say it regretfully), it is a question of the aroused heart which the miraculous and common flesh recovers, and which can at every instant stop fighting and reconciling.

Translations from René Char

XVI

Between *your* greatest good and *their* least evil blushes poetry.

XVII

The swarm, the lightning flash and the anathema—three angles of the same summit.

XVIII

To stay firmly on the ground, and, with love, to give your arm to a fruit not accepted by those who support you, to set up what one thinks is his house, without the help of the first stone, which always inconceivably goes wrong, that is *the curse.*

XIX

Do not complain about living closer to death than those destined to die.

XX

Seemingly one is always born half-way between the beginning and the end of the world. We add to our stature in open revolt almost as furiously against what drags us away as against what holds us back.

XXI

Imitate men as little as possible in their enigmatic sickness of tying knots.

XXII

Death is detestable only because it affects each one of our five senses separately, then all at once. At a pinch, the ear would ignore it.

XXIII

One does not build *multiformly* except by mistake. This is what permits us, with each springtide, to imagine ourselves happy.

XXIV

When the ship sinks, its sails survive, within us. They are hoisted on the mast of our blood. Their fresh impatience draws itself up for other obstinate voyages. It's you, isn't it, who is blind on the sea? You who vacillate in all this blueness, O sadness raised up on the farthest waves?

XXV

We are passersby intent on passing by, thence to spreading trouble, inflicting our heat, uttering our exuberance. That is why we intervene! That is why we are unseasonable and unwonted! Our crest is nothing. Our usefulness is turned against the employer.

XXVI

I can despair of myself and yet sustain my hope in You. I have fallen from my splendour, and death seen by everyone, you take no note of it, fern in the wall, walking on my arm.

XXVII

If finally you destroy yourself, let it be with nuptial tools.

Translations from René Char
173

LASCAUX

DEAD BIRD-MAN AND DYING BISON

Long body which was voraciously enthusiastic,
Now perpendicular to the wounded Beast.

O disembowelled victim!
Victim of she who was all and, reconciled, now dies;
He, dancer over the abyss, spirit, ever to be born,
Magic's cruelly preserved bird and perverse fruit.

BLACK STAGS

The waters were murmuring to the sky.
Stags, you have crossed a thousand years of space
From the rock's darkness to the air's gentle touch.

From my broad shore, how much I love the passion
Of the hunter who drives you on and the spirit who watches over
     you!
And what if I had their eyes, this moment I hope for them?

JOHN THOMPSON
174

THE UNNAMABLE BEAST

The unnamable Beast brings up the rear of the graceful herd like a
    clownish cyclops.
Eight jibing barbs adorn her, stake out her buffoonery.
The Beast lows devotedly in the country air.
Her stuffed, sagging flanks are painful, about to disgorge their
    fullness.
A humid stench clings to her, from her hoof to her useless horns.

Thus appeared to me in the Lascaux frieze, this fantastically
    disguised mother,
Wisdom with her eyes full of tears.

YOUNG HORSE WITH THE MISTY MANE

How beautiful you are in the spring, horse,
Combing the sky with your mane,
Covering the reeds with foam!
All of love has its home in your breast:
From the White Lady of Africa
To Magdalene at her mirror,
The combatant idol, and contemplative grace.

Translations from René Char
175

FEVER OF PETITE-PIERRE, ALSACE

We advanced through the blazing stretch of forest as the ship's bow heads into the waves, swelling tide of nights, now given up to the union of explosion and destruction. Behind this savage wall, beyond this ceiling, retreat of a stentor reduced to silence and fervor, is there a sky?

We saw it at the same moment that the village came into view, masonry of dawn and nonchalant evening, riding at anchor in expectation of our tide.

Persistent leaps, fruitful march, we are at once the roadsteads and the mainsail of the everyday sea at grips with the lines, to infinity, of ships. You teach it to us, undergrowth. Just as the mortal fire is crossed.

PASSAGE TO LYON

I'll come by the bridge furthest from Bellecour, so as to give you the freedom of arriving first. You'll take me to the window from which your eyes set out, from which your favors plunge when your liberty exchanges its light with the meteors', yours lasting, theirs dissolving. With my dreams, with my war, with my kiss, under the revived mulberry bush, during a pause in the spinning, I'll do my best to cut off your conquest from a former knowledge, other than mine. That the future might lead you away with others who lust, I concede—but for the unique masterpiece.

Flame at the peak of its destiny, sometimes withering me and sometimes bringing my fulfillment, you emerge instantaneously, close to me, princess, salamander, and I am nothing to you.

THE EDGE OF TROUBLE

All hands on a stone,
Purple hands, docile hands,
For two activists who distill.

Hands, in sublime weather, which the air supports at the same
    instant as the arch:
Given to my heaviness by the perfume of the swamp-iris
One misty evening, from their side.
            (Paris, Musée Rodin)

MUTTERINGS

So as not to yield myself, and to find myself again, I offend you, but
what a passion I have for you, wolf, so-called with funereal wrong,
fat with the secrets of my back-country. It is in a mass of legendary
love that you leave the virginal shreds, garnered by your claw. Wolf is
what I call you, but you have no nameable reality. Moreover, you are
unintelligible. Non-comparing, compensator, what do I know? Be-
hind your wiry lope, I bleed, I weep, I am stiff with terror, I forget, I
laugh under the trees. Merciless hunt, tenaciously prosecuted, where
everything is put into action against the double prey: you invisible
and me full of life.

Keep on, keep going, we shall endure together; and together, though
separated, we shall leap across the shudder of the supreme deception
to break the ice of living waters, and there salute each other in rec-
ognition.

Translations from René Char

THE RISK AND THE PENDULUM

You who gather yourself up and pass between the flourishing blossom and the acrobat, be the one for whom the butterfly alights on the wayside flowers.

Stay with the wave the moment its heart expires. You will see.

Sensitive also to the saliva of the twig.

With no more choice between forgetting and learning well.

May you keep your essential friends to windward of your branch.

She carries the word, the pioneering bee who, through hatreds and ambushes, goes to lay her honey on the passing caprice of a cloud.

The night is no longer astonished by the blind which man draws.

A dust which falls on the hand engaged in composing a poem, shatters them both, poem and hand.

IN ORDER TO RENEW

We have suddenly come too close to something from which we had been kept at a mysteriously favorable and rhythmic distance. Since when, corrosion. Our head-rest has disappeared.

It is intolerable to feel oneself an integral and important part of a beauty in the process of dying by default of others. Integral with its breast, and impotent in the movement of its spirit.

If what I show you and what I give you seem less than what I hide from you, my balance is poor, my gleaning without virtue.

You are the altar of darkness on my too freely revealed face, poem. My magnificence and my suffering have slipped between the two.

Throw off this so foully accumulated existence and recover the look which loved it enough, when it began, to lay out its foundations. What's left to me to live lies in this assault, in this thrill.

TIDE'S REPORT

Have earth and sky renounced their seasonal enchantments, their pervasive palavers? Have they submitted? The former no more than the latter has, it seems, further plans for them, nor happiness for us.

A branch awakens to the gilded words of the lamp, a branch in ditch-water, a bough without a future. The glance fastens onto it, moves on. Then, once again, everything languishes, patient, in balance and suffering. The acantha plays dead. But, this time, we shall not take the road together.

Beloved, behind my door?

INVITATION

I summon the loves which, broken and pursued by the summer's scythe, sweeten the evening air with the perfume of their white pros-tration.

There is no more nightmare, sweet perpetual insomnia. No more aversion. Only the brief interlude in the dance whose entrance is everywhere in the sky's large clouds.

I come before the clamouring of the fountains, with the stone-cut-ter's finale.

One death weighs more heavily on my lyre than a thousand years.

I summon the lovers.

THE LIBRARY IS ON FIRE

It is snowing from the muzzle of this cannon. Hell was in our head. At the same instant it is spring at our finger-tips. It is the newly permitted stride, the earth in love, the exuberant grass.

The spirit also, like everything else, has shuddered.

The eagle is for the future.

Every action that involves the soul, though the soul were unaware of it, will have repentance or chagrin as an epilogue. We must consent to this.

How did writing come to me? Like bird's-down on my winter window-pane. Immediately, in the hearth, there flared up a battle of firebrands which has not, up to now, come to an end.

Silky towns with a humdrum air, in among other towns, with streets followed by us alone, under the wing of lightning flashes which respond to our expectancy.

Everything in us should be nothing but a joyous festival when something we have not foreseen, which we cannot throw light on, which is going to speak to our hearts, unaided, is accomplished.

Let us continue to take soundings, to speak with a steady voice, with tight-knit words, we shall finish by silencing all these dogs, by getting them to confuse themselves with the grass, keeping watch on us with a smoky eye while the wind wipes out their backs.

For me the lightning flash endures.

Only my fellow-beings, my companions — men or women — can rouse me from my torpor, unleash my poetry, thrust me against the limits of the ancient desert so that I can triumph. Nothing else. Neither heaven nor the privileged earth, nor the things at which one shudders. A torch, I dance only with them.

One cannot begin a poem without a fragment of error concerning himself and the world, without a wisp of innocence in the first words.

In the poem, each, or almost each word should be used in its original meaning. Some of them, cutting loose, may become plurivalent. And there are amnesiac ones. The constellation of the solitary is arrayed.

Poetry will steal my death from me.

Why *pulverized poem*? Because at the end of its journey towards the Homeland, after the prenatal darkness and earth's harshness, the finitude of the poem is light, what being bears into life.

The poet does not keep back what he discovers; recording it, he soon loses it. In this lies his freshness, his infiniteness and his peril.

My craft is a craft of the arrow-point.

One is born among men, one dies unconsoled with the gods.

The earth receiving the seed is sad. The seed, which is going to risk so much, is happy.

There is a kind of curse unlike any other. It flutters almost indolently, as it were, has a pleasing nature, affects a reassuring expression. But, the deception over, how resilient it is, how directly it makes for its goal. Probably, for the darkness where it acts is evil, the region perfectly secret, it will elude a summons, will always slip away in time.

JOHN THOMPSON
182

It traces frightening parables in the shroud of the sky of a few clair-
voyants.

Stagnant books. But books which, these days, subtly insinuate them-
selves, heave a sigh, perform the opening of dances.

How to express my liberty, my surprise, at the end of a thousand
detours: there is no ground, there is no ceiling.

From time to time the silhouette of a young horse, of a far-off child,
comes scouting towards me and leaps the barrier of my anxiety. Then
under the trees the fountain speaks once again.

We want to stay hidden from the curiosity of those who love us. We
love them.

The light has an age. The night does not. But what was the instant
of this entire beginning?

Do not have several deaths in suspension and as though snowed in.
Have only one, of good sand. And without resurrection.

Let us keep close to those who can cut themselves off from their
resources, even though there exists for them little or no falling back.
Waiting deepens in them a vertiginous insomnia. Beauty adorns them
with a hat of flowers.

You birds who entrust your slenderness, your perilous sleep, to a
clump of reeds — come the cold, how like you we are!

I admire the hands which are full and the finger which, to mate, to
join, throws off the thimble.

I sometimes warn myself that the current of our existence is hardly
to be grasped; since we suffer not only its capricious nature, but the

facile movement of arms and legs which would make us go there where we would be happy to go, on the coveted bank, to encounter loves whose differences would enrich us, this movement remains incomplete, its image swiftly fading, like a drop of perfume on our thought.

Desire, desire that knows, we shall not draw advantage from our shadows, except after several real, harmonious sovereignties of invisible flames, of invisible chains, which revealing themselves, step by step, make us shine.

Beauty makes its sublime bed quite alone, strangely builds its renown among men, beside them, but apart.

Let us sow the reeds and cultivate the vine on the hillsides, beside the wounds of our spirit. Cruel fingers, cautious hands, this jocular place is propitious.

He who invents, as opposed to him who discovers, adds nothing to things, brings to beings only masks, partitions, metallic gruel.

At last the whole of life, when I pluck the delicacy of your loving truth from your depths.

Stay close to the cloud. Watch closely over the tool. All seed is detested.

Beneficence of men on certain shrill mornings. In the seething of the delirious air, I climb, I seal myself up, undevoured insect, pursued and pursuing.

Facing these waters, harsh forms, where all the flowers of the green mountain pass in glittering bouquets, the Hours are wed to gods.

Cool sun, whose liana I am.

THE COMPANIONS IN THE GARDEN

Man is simply a flower of the air gripped by the earth, damned by the stars, sucked in by death; on occasion, the breath and shadow of this coalition raise him up.

Our friendship is the white cloud preferred by the sun.

Our friendship is a free rind. It does not detach itself from the prowess of our heart.

When the spirit no longer uproots but transplants and tends, I am born. When the childhood of the people begins, I love.

20th century: man was completely unbalanced. Women became enlightened and moved about swiftly, on an overhang which only our eyes could reach.

I bind myself to a rose.

We are ungovernable. The only master who looks on us with favor is the Lightning Flash, which sometimes illuminates us and sometimes cuts us in two.

Just as they fade, the lightning flash and the rose unite in us for our fulfillment.

I am grass in your hand, my adolescent pyramid. I make love to you on your thousand flowers once more closed.

Lend all the brilliance of the deep flower to the bud, leaving there its future. Your hard second look can do this. This way, the frost will not destroy it.

Translations from René Char

Let us not allow anyone to take away from us the part of nature we enclose within us. Let us not lose one stamen of it nor yield one drop of water.

After the departure of the reapers, on the plateaus of the Ile-de-France, this fragile chiselled flint which comes out of the earth, scarcely in our hand, brings surging into our memory a corresponding stone: kernel of a dawn of which, we believe, we shall see neither the decline nor the end; only its sublime crimson and uplifted face.

Their crime: a raging desire to teach us to scorn the gods we have within us.

It is pessimists who are spawned by the future. They see the object of their anxiety realised in their lifetime. However, with the passing of the harvest, the grape-bunch bends over the vine stock; and the children of the seasons, who have not come together in the usual way, pack down as quickly as possible the sand by the side of the wave. This the pessimists perceive also.

Ah, the power to rise up re-formed.

Tell us, will what we are make us burst out into a bouquet?

A poet should leave traces of his passing, not proofs. Only traces provoke the dream.

Living — is it a determined effort to consummate a memory? Dying — is it becoming, though *nowhere*, alive?

The real sometimes fulfills hope. That is why, against all expectations, hope survives.

To cast one's shadow across the dunghill — so glutted is our flesh with ills, and our hearts with mad thoughts — that is possible; but sustain within yourself something sacred.

When I dream and when I move forward, when I grasp the ineffable, awaking, I am on my knees.

History is only the reverse side of the stance of leaders. Also a land of fear where the she-wolf hunts and the viper rasps. Distress shows in the glance of human societies and Time, as the victories increase.

Gleaming and thrusting forward — swift knife, slow star.

In the shattering of the universe we experience, wonder! The clashing fragments are *alive*.

My whole earth, like a bird become fruit in an eternal tree, I am yours.

What your winters ask of us is to bear up into the air what would otherwise be only scraps and the butt of insults. What your winters ask of us is to be for you a prelude to savour: a savour equal to that sung by the civilization of fruit under its winged roundness.

What consoles me is that when I am dead I shall be there — broken, hideous — to see myself as poem.

My lyre does not have to divine my nature, nor my poetry be what I could have written.

The marvellous nature of this being: in him, every spring gives birth to a stream. With the least of his gifts a shower of doves descends.

In our gardens forests are readying themselves.

Free birds do not tolerate being watched. When near them, let us keep to the shadows, denying ourselves.

O yet survive, always better.

GOOD GRACE OF AN APRIL TIME

TO TWO CHILDREN

1.

I have seen your twenty-day-old blue eyes
Give a clear shimmer to the leaves
of the elm and the tamarisk.

I have seen your father stretch tall
Lifting you onto his breast
And your mother's shape in silhouette
Kissing your soft seaweed cheeks.

In the mollifying cradle
Where you blush, little dawn,
Elizabeth, I discover you
Like a rose in the undergrowth.

And that makes me happy,
I, walker in the delicate rain.

2.

　　　Helen,
With the slow cradle, the docile horse,
Good day! My inn is yours.

How subtle is your warmth
Which knows, obliquely, how to find my heart,
Dear child of streams, of dreamers,
　　　Helen! Helen!

JOHN THOMPSON
188

But what do they wish of you, the seasons
Who love you in four ways?
That your beauty, this light
Should enter and pass through every house?
Or that the ever full moon
Should take you and enwrap your hand
Until the love that you demand?

THE HIGHWAY OF SEALS

Curls, according to the look,
Simple desire of the word;
Ah! juggle, dominion of the neck
With the sovereign mouth,
with the lighted faggot
Beneath the imposing brow.

I would like to be able to lie to you
As the glowing coals lie to the ashes,
Curls, heedlessly flying
Over a momentary stage.

EPITAPH

Lifted by the bird from scattered grief,
And left to the forests for a work of love.

THE STRUCK TREE

The spacious lightning and the fire of the kiss
Will exchange my tomb raised by the storm.

THE PALACES AND THE HOUSES

Today Paris is reached. I shall live there. My arm will no longer hurl my soul into the distance. I belong.

IN SPACE

The sun was flying low, as low as the bird. The night extinguished them both. I loved them.

IT IS TRULY HER

Land of base night and torments.

*

Night, my foliage and my soil.

THE IRON GATE

I am not alone because I am abandoned. I am alone because I am alone, an almond within the walls of its shell.

THE GODS ARE BACK

The Gods are back, comrades. They have just now penetrated into this life; but the word which revokes, under the word which unfolds, it also has reappeared to make us suffer together.

ARTINE IN THE ECHO

Our sumptuous entanglement in the body of the milky way, summit bedchamber for our couple who elsewhere in the night would freeze.

LULLABY FOR EACH DAY UNTIL THE LAST

Numerous times, a good many times,
Man falls asleep, his body wakes him;
Then once, only once,
Man falls asleep and loses his body.

TO MINE

I come into contact with an area and I can set it on fire. I husband my stature, I know how to unleash it. But what is desire without your jealous swarm? The buttercup is lusterless without the tint of the meadows.

When you suddenly appear, my hand will call upon you, my hand, the still living little monster. But, except for you, what beauty? . . . what beauty?

THE WARBLER IN THE REEDS

The tree most exposed to the eye of the rifle is not the tree for her wing. The restless one has been alerted: she will stay dumb while passing through it. The willow perch is shattered the moment the fugitive's claw leaves it. But once in the reeds, what cavatinas she sings. The whole world knows it.

Summer, river, space, deceived lovers, a whole moon of water, the warbler repeats: "Free, free, free, free . . ."

Translations from René Char

191

MORTAL REMAINS AND MOZART

In the half-light of morning, only once, the old unpeopled pink cloud will fly over the henceforth distant eyes, in the majesty of its unimpeded slowness; then will come the cold, the immense possessor, and Time which has no place.

Along his two lips, on common ground, suddenly, the allegro, challenge of this sacred outcast, breaks through and surges back toward the living, toward the totality of the men and women mourning the interior homeland, who, wandering so as not to be alike, pass through Mozart to test themselves in secret.

— Beloved, when you dream aloud and by chance pronounce my name, tender conqueror of our shared fears, of my solitary disrepute, the night is luminous to cross.

THE ONE AND THE OTHER

Why must you endlessly sway, rosebush, throughout the long rain,
    with your double rose?
Like two full-grown wasps they remain, not flying.
I see them with my heart, for my eyes are closed.
Above the flowers, my love has left only wind and cloud.

GOAD

"Why this ardour, young face?"
"I'm leaving, the summer is swept away.
With bold strokes my fear tells me so,
Better than the gray water and the bees."
"Knees to fists, alerted angel;
My whip cracks on your wing."

ON AN UNADORNED NIGHT

See the night beaten to death; continue our self-sufficiency in it.

In the night, poet, drama and nature are bound together as one, but climbing and drawing their own breath.

The night bears nourishment, the sun pares down the nourished one.

In the night our apprenticeships keep themselves ready to be useful to others after us. Fertile is the freshness of this guardian.

The infinite attacks but a cloud saves.

The night affiliates itself with whatever instance of life is prepared to end in spring, to fly thunderously.

The night becomes rust-colored when it consents to half-open the gates of its gardens for us.

Compared with the living night, the dream is sometimes only a spectral lichen.

Translations from René Char

We shouldn't have set the heart of the night on fire. The master had to be darkness, where the morning dew is chiselled.

The night gives way only to itself. The solar tocsin is merely tolerated by the night — from self-interest.

It is the night that undertakes the task of escorting back our mystery; it is the night that performs the toilet of the elect.

The night destroys the illusions of our human past, bows down its psyche before the present, puts indecision into our future.

I shall fill myself with a heavenly earth.

Fullness of night where the ungracious dream no longer blinks, keep what I love alive for me.

CONTIGUITIES

The meadows tell me stream
And the streams meadow.

The wind stays in the cloud.
My zeal is the weather's coolness.

But the bee is dreamy
And the roach slides under the mud.
The bird does not stop.

CAPTIVES

In play my youth took life prisoner
O dungeon where I live!

Fields, you gaze upon yourselves in my four harvests,
I thunder, you turn.

THE SPIRITUAL BIRD

Do not implore me, large eyes; stay in hiding, desires.
I disappear into the sky, ponds without thresholds.
I glide in freedom through the ripe corn.
No breath clouds the mirror of my flight.
I pursue human misfortune, strip from it the flesh of
  its leisure.

Translations from René Char

LINE OF FAITH

The beneficence of the stars is to invite us to speak, to
show us that we are not alone, that the dawn has a roof
and my fire your two hands.

THE OUTCOME

Everything was extinguished:
The day, the inner light,
A mass of pain,
I no longer found my true time,
My home.

The pacing of the insufficiently dead
Rang in all the voids;
I confined myself
To a cloudy sky.

Nourished by what is not of the place,
Step by step, almost consoled.

The vine will be full
Where your shoulder struggles,
Safe and same sun.

THE OPEN STRIDE OF RENÉ CREVEL

But what if words are spades?

Then death, down below, will have caught only your echo.
Your buckled word always mingles with the vapour we breathe
    from our mouths
When winter scatters its hoar-frost on our cloaks.
The spirit does not want to harden into stone
And struggles with the mud which presses it to such an attempt.
But sleep, sleep is a parsimonious spade.
Oh, let him who wishes to leave, disappear into the night which
    grief no longer abuses.

FOR A SAXIFRAGE PROMETHEUS
while touching the Aeolian hand of Hölderlin

Reality without the dislocating energy of poetry, what is that?

God had lived too powerfully among us. We no longer knew how to
get up and leave. In our eyes they had died, those stars which were
sovereign in his gaze.

These are the angel questions which provoked the invasion of demons.
They fasten us to the rock to beat us and to love us. Once more.

The struggle itself takes place in the darkness. Victory is found only
at the edges.

Noble seed, war and favor of my fellow-being, before the deaf dawn
I keep you with my hunk of bread, waiting for the foretold day of
heavy rain, of green mud, which will come for the fiery ones and for
the obstinate.

Translations from René Char
197

FLORA'S STAIRCASE

Why, most alive of all the living, are you
only shadows of flowers among the living?

Raw-silk heat, thundering morrow, you who
will touch land before me, ah! do not cast
aside what will soon be a mass of love for you.

THE WAY ALONG THE PATHS

The paths, those ruts which run invisibly beside the highway, are our
unique way; they are for us who speak in order to live, who sleep,
without becoming numb, on our sides.

DECLARING HIS NAME

I was ten. The Sorgue enshrined me. The sun sang the hours on the
wise sun-dial of the waters. Unconcern and grief had sealed up the
iron cock on the roofs of houses and together they endured each
other. But in the heart of the watchful child what wheel turned more
powerfully, more swiftly than that of the mill in its white blazing?

TRAVERSE

The hill which he has done well by runs in a torrent down his spine.
The poor tongues greet him; the mules in the field fête him. The
pink face of the rut turns the wave of its mirror toward him twice.
Spitefulness sleeps. He is as he dreamed himself to be.

IF . . .

We will never again be repatriated. We will no longer stretch our
limbs; we will die no more in a fabulous distant land. The sky has
decayed, as far as its most distant rainbow; no look can rekindle it.
The earth is like a devotionless heap of bones.

OF 1943

You have indeed profited yourself in our souls,
Old sleep of putrefaction!

Since then,
Moon after day,
Wind after night,
Frail or strong,
We wait.

THE RAISED SCYTHE

When the drover of the dead raps with his staff,
Dedicate my scattered color to the summer.
Amaze a child with my too blue fists.
Arrange on his cheeks my lamp and my gleanings.

Spring, pulsing through your narrowed channels,
Lavish my gains on the thirsts of the fields.
From the moist fern to the feverish mimosa,
Between the old man who is absent and the newcomer,
Love's movement, bending down, will say to you:
"There is no other place, disgrace is everywhere."

Translations from René Char

THE UNPREDICTED FUTURE

I watch you living in a celebration which my fear of coming to an end leaves obscure.

Our hands close upon a flagellant star. The reed-flute is to be sharpened again.

The tip of a brutal sun barely touches a newly beginning day.

No longer knowing if so much victorious sap ought to sing or remain silent, I have unclenched the fist of Time and seized its harvest.

There appeared a manifold and sterile rainbow.

Solar Eve, possibility of flesh and dust, I do not believe in the unveiling of others, but in yours alone.

Who scolds, let him follow me right to our portals.

I feel my new breath being born and my grief ending.

EROS SUSPENDED

The night had run half its course. The masses of the skies, at this moment, were about to be held completely in my gaze. I saw you, the first and only one, divine female in the overthrown spheres. I stripped off your robe of infinity, brought you back naked onto my earth. The mobile soil of the land was everywhere.

We fly, say your servants, in cruel space, — to the song of my red trumpet.

WE ARE FALLING

My brevity is not fettered.

Sustaining kisses. Your scattered fragments suddenly form a
dulled body.

O my unnatural avalanche!

Completely bound.

Like a supper in the wind.

Completely bound. Returned to the air.

Like a reddened road along the cliff. A fleeting animal.

The depth of impatience and vertical patience intermingled.

The dance turned back. The warring whip.

Your limpid eyes grown large.

These light immortal words never plunged into mourning.

Ivy in its silent rows.

Frond which the sea approached. Counter-cut of the day.

Lower your weight again.

Death beats us with the back of its fork. Until a sober morning
appear in us.

THE RISING OF THE NIGHT

I double the petals and darken the corolla of the flower that I nourish.

Time rips and slashes. A gleam moves away from it: our knife.

Spring takes you captive and winter frees you, land of the leaps of love
.
The star gives up to me the wasp sting that was buried in her.

Watch, bowed face, you irrigate the hearts of the goats on the peaks.

TO LEAVE

WE HAVE

Our word, in archipelago, offers you, after grief and disaster, straw-berries which it brings back from the wastelands of the dead, warm, just as its fingers warm from seeking them.

Deltaless tyrannies, on which noon never casts light, for you we are the declining day; but you are not aware that we are also the voracious, though veiled, eye of the origin.

To make a poem is to take possession of a nuptial beyond which, to be sure, is grounded in this life, is inextricably bound up with it, and yet lies close to the burial urn.

We must get outside ourselves, at the edge of tears and in the orbit of famines, if we want something out of the ordinary to happen, which would be for us alone.

If the anguish which empties us out abandoned its icy cave, if the beloved in our heart stopped the rain of ants, the Song would begin again.

In the chaos of an avalanche, two stones, wedded in flight, could make love naked in space. The sea of snow which engulfed them would be amazed by the passion of their moss.

Man was surely the most insane wish of the darkness; that is why we are shadowy, envious and mad under the powerful sun.

An earth which was beautiful has commenced her death-struggle, under the gaze of her fluttering sisters, in the presence of her insensate sons.

Translations from René Char

We have in us vast areas where we will never succeed in planting our heels; but they are useful in our harsh climate, and beneficial to our vigilance as well as our perditions.

How can we throw back into darkness our former heart and its right to return?

Poetry is that ripened fruit which we gaily grasp in our hand at the very moment it appears to us; its future uncertain, on the frosted stem, in the flower's calyx.

Poetry, man's unique ascension, which the sun of the dead cannot darken in the perfect and burlesque infinite.

*

With a mystery more powerful than their curse making their hearts innocent, they planted a tree in Time, and Time became their lover.

ON THE MARCH

This incessant and phosphorescent trailing after itself of death which we read in the eyes of those who love us, without wishing to hide it from them.

Must we distinguish between a hideous death and a death prepared by the hand of genius? Between a death with the face of a beast and a death with the face of death?

*

We can live only in the half-open, exactly on the hermetic line which divides the darkness and the light. But we are irresistibly thrown forward. All our being lends aid and dizziness to this thrust.

*

Poetry is at once utterance and silent provocation, despairing of the constant demand of our being for the appearance of an unrivalled reality. She is incorruptible. Not imperishable; for she runs all the risks. But the only one who visibly triumphs over material death. Such is Beauty, Beauty of the high seas, which has appeared since the first ages of our heart, sometimes derisively conscious, sometimes luminously informed.

What inspires my sympathy, what I love, soon causes me almost as much suffering as that from which I turn away, resisting, in the mystery of my heart: veiled affectations of a tear.

The only signature at the foot of the white life is the poetry which shapes it. And always between our burst heart and the revealed cascade.

For the dawn, disgrace is the day to come; for the twilight the night which engulfs it. Formerly there were people of the dawn. Here we are, perhaps, at this hour of nightfall. But why crested like larks?

Translations from René Char

ETERNITY AT LOURMARIN
ALBERT CAMUS

There is no longer a straight line nor a lamp-lit path with a being who has left us. Where is our affection stunned? Ripple after ripple, if he approaches it is immediately to flee. From time to time his face comes to press itself up against ours, producing only an icy brightness. The day which increased the happiness between him and us has gone completely. All the parts — almost excessive — of a presence have been dislocated at one stroke. Routine of our vigilance . . . However, this suppressed being is held in something solid, solitary, essential in us, where all our millennia together make up only the thickness of one stretched eyelid.

We have ceased to speak with him who we love, but there is not silence. What, then, is there? We know, or believe we know. But only when the meaningful past opens up to give him passage. Then he is at our height, then distant, ahead of us.

At a time once more oppressive, when we are examining the whole weight of the enigma, grief suddenly begins, that of companion for companion, which the archer, this time, does not transfix.

ALONG THE BANKS OF SORGUE

The spaceman whose birthday it is today will be a thousand million times less luminous and will reveal a thousand million fewer hidden things than the man of granite, recluse and sleeper of Lascaux, his stiff member cleansed of death.

TO CONTRAVENE

Obey your swine who exist. I submit to my gods who do not exist.

We remain inclement people.

THE PEAKS OF MONTMIRAIL

At the summit of the mountain, among the pebbles, the trumpets of baked earth
of the men of old white frosts were cheeping like young eagles.

If there is to be grief, let it be harsh.

Poetry thrives on perpetual insomnia.

It seems that the sky has the last word. But it speaks in such a low
voice that no one ever hears it.

There is no withdrawal, only a millennial patience on which we are
leaning.

Sleep, you who despair; soon it will be day — a winter's day.

With death we have only one recourse: to make art before it.

Reality cannot be crossed unless it is raised up.

In times of distress and improvisation, some are killed only for a
night and others for eternity: song of the lark of the entrails.

The quest for a brother almost always means the search for a being,
our equal, to whom we wish to offer the transcendences whose signs
we have only just finished deciphering.

Translations from René Char

The upright tomb: a corn-stook. Grain for the bread, straw for the dung-hill.

Watch only once the wave throw its anchor into the sea.

The imaginary is not pure; it only provokes movement.

The great perpetuate themselves only through the great. One forgets. Only moderation is wounded.

What kind of swimmer is he who does not know how to slide completely under the waters?

Fists clenched to hit make poor hands to work.

Savage rains favor deep passersby.

The essential is what escorts us, at the desired time, along the way. It is also a dim lamp in the smoke.

The writing of a blue flare, hurried, jagged, intrepid, of the then infant Mount Ventoux, flashed always across the horizon of Montmirail which at every moment our love brought me, inspired me.

Debris of kings of an impregnable ferocity.

The clouds have intentions as enigmatic as those of men.

It is not the stomach which craves good hot soup, but the heart.

Sleep in the wound like salt.

An unnamable interference has taken away from things, from circumstances, from beings, their fortuitous halo. There is no advent for us beyond this halo. It does not immunize.

This snow: we loved it; it had no path, it revealed our hunger.

ALLÉGRESSE

The clouds are in the rivers, the torrents rush across the sky. Unless plucked the days run to seed, die unripened. The time of famine and that of harvest, one under the other in the tattered air, have effaced their difference. They flow together, they bivouac. How should fear be distinguished from hope, furrowed highways? The houses no longer have thresholds, the clearings no smoke. The desire for warmth has fallen into the abyss — and this small obscurity at our back where the primrose was troubled as soon as the future espied it.

Bridge on the invasion route, exposed to the conqueror, relenting to defeat. Will we know, under the heel of death, that the heart, this sheaver, must not precede, but follow?

FONTIS

The grape has for homeland
The fingers of the gatherer.
But she, who has she,
Beyond the narrow track of the cruel vineyard?

The rosary of the bunch of grapes;
In the evening the highest reclining fruit which bleeds

The last spark.

PRECURSOR

to Yves de Bayser

In a rock, I recognized fleeting and measurable death, the open bed of his small mute attendants in the shelter of a fig tree. No sign of quarrying; each of earth's mornings spread its wings at the foot of night's steps.

Without repeating myself, unburdened of man's fear, I hollow out in the air my tomb and my return.

AT THE GATES OF AEREA

The joyous time. Each city was one large family united by fear; the song of hands at their work and the sky's lively night illumined them. The pollen of the spirit kept to its role of exile.

But the perpetual present, the instantaneous past, under the master fatigue, removed the guard-rails.

Forced march, with limited ends. Beaten children, gilded cottage, ulcerous men, all on the rack.

Picked out by the iron bee, the weeping rose opened.

THE FIG TREE'S LIED

It froze so much that the milky branches
Damaged the saw, broke up in one's hands.
Spring does not live to green the elegant.

The fig tree asked the master of felled timber
For the bush of a new faith.
But the oriole, its prophet,
Alighting on the disaster
In the warm dawn of its return,
Perished not from hunger but from love.

IN PRAISE OF GIACOMETTI

One late afternoon in April 1964, the old despotic eagle, the kneeling shoe-smith, under the flaming cloud of his invective (he ceaselessly lashes his work, that is himself, with contempt), revealed to me, down on the tiled floor of his studio, the image of Caroline, his model, Caroline's face painted on canvas — after how many scratches, wounds, bloodclots? —, fruit of a passion between all the objects of love, victorious with the false gigantism of the summed scraps of death, and also the barely separated glistening particles of us others, his temporal witnesses. Outside his sombre cell of desire and cruelty. It was reflected, this beautiful ancestorless face which would kill sleep, in the mirror of our gaze, provisional universal receiver for all future eyes.

Translations from René Char

ALSATIAN REGIONS

I showed you La Petite-Pierre, its forest's dowry, the sky being
    born between the branches,
Its flocks of birds, hunters of other birds,
The twice-living pollen under the flowers' blaze,
A tower in the distance hoisted like the sail of a privateer,
The lake once more the mill's cradle, a child's sleep.

There where my sash of snow lies heavy on me,
Under the overhang of a rock dotted with crows,
I have left the need for winter.
Today we love each other without beyond and without issue,
Passionate or withdrawn, different but together,
Diverting each other with stars whose nature is to fly without
    arriving.

The ship is bound for the vegetal high sea.
All fires out, it takes us aboard.
In its recollection, we were taken on just before dawn.
It sheltered our childhood, ballasted our golden age,
The summoned, the wandering host, just as much as we believe in
    its truth.

NEEDLE MIRAGE

They take the yellow laughter of the darkness for light. They test the weight of death's remains in their hands, and cry: "Not for us!" No precious viaticum adorns the jaws of their uncoiled serpents. Their wives deceive them, their children leave home, their friends jeer at them. They see nothing of this, because they hate darkness. Does the diamond of the creation throw off flames at all angles? Immediately, they cover it with a lure. They put into their ovens, add to the sleek dough of their bread, only a pinch of wheaty despair. They have established themselves and prosper in the cradle of a sea in which one has become master of glaciers. You are forewarned.

Feeble schoolboy, how will you convert the future and douse this much questioned, much stirred fire which has fallen across your faulty gaze?

The present is only a game or a massacre of archers.

Since then, faithful to his love as the sky is to the rock. Faithful, charred, but perpetually wandering, stealing his way through the whole visible extent of the fire, held in the wind, this area, butcher's treasure bleeding on a hook.

THE LOST NUDE

Those whose endurance knows how to make use of the knotty night which precedes and follows the light will become palm-bearers. Their utterance owes its existence to the intermittent fruit which propagates it by splitting itself apart.

They are the incestuous sons of the notch and the scar who lifted up onto the well-brim the water-jar's flowered girth. The fury of the wind still keeps them stripped naked. Against them flies a feather of black night.

Translations from René Char

TO CHERISH THOUZON

When grief had hoisted him onto his coveted roof, an obvious knowledge revealed itself to him quite unobscured. He was no longer situated in his liberty like two oars in mid-ocean. The captivating desire for utterance had receded with the black waters. Persisting here and there were slight tremors whose fading wakes he followed. A half-masked granite dove spanned the sparse vestiges of the sunken great work with its wings. On the humid slopes, wisps of foam and the indigent trail of broken shapes. In the stringent epoch which began, the privilege of gathering the harvest unpoisoned was abolished. All the wild and free streams of the creation had completely stopped running. At the end of his life he would have to yield up to the new audacity what an immense patience had, with each dawn, allowed him.

The day revolved over Thouzon. Death has not like the lichen cut down the snow's hope. In the well of the sunken town, the moon's sickle-point stirred the last blood into the first mud.

HOSPITABLE THIRST

Who ever heard her complain?

No one but she could have drunk the forty exhaustions without
    dying,
And waited, far ahead, for those who afterwards would submit;
From dawn to dusk her workmanship was like a man's.

Whoever has sunk the well and draws the helpless water
Risks his heart in the spreading of her hands.

TRACED ON THE ABYSS

I watched you suffering in the chimerical plague of Vaucluse. There, although cast down, you were a green water, and still a path. You were passing through death in its disorder. Undulating flower of a continuing secret.

THE LEFT-HANDED

One doesn't console himself for nothing when he walks holding a hand, the risky floraison of a hand's flesh.

The darkness of the hand which squeezes us and drags us along, innocent enough, the sweet-smelling hand where we add to our stature and husband our resources, not evading the ravine or the thornbush, the untimely fire, the encroachment of men, this hand preferred above all, lifts us from the shadow's duplication, from evening into day. Into the day shining above evening, its threshold of agony bruised.

WITH BRAQUE, PERHAPS IT WAS THOUGHT

When the snow falls asleep, the night calls off its dogs.

Fruits, you stay so far from your tree that the stars in the sky seem to be your reflection.

We go astray when the straight path, which is imprinted ahead of us, becomes the ground we tread on. We debase ourselves to a wretched felicity.

Savour of waves which do not recede. They thrust the sea back into its past.

Translations from René Char

The blood lives in the arrow's feathers, not on its point. The bow wanted it thus.

The storm has two houses. One occupies a small spot on the horizon; as to the other, a whole man could barely contain it.

The dew suffers immediately. Throughout foul mornings it contends with the night's hypogeum, the day's brashness, and the spring's lasting tumult.

This man was covered with the bites of his imagination. The imaginary bleeds only from old scars.

Art is a road which ends in a footpath, a springboard, though in a field which is ours.

THE BRITTLE AGE

I was born like the rock, with my wounds. Without curing my superstitious youth, exhausted by limpid resolution, I will enter the brittle age.

In the present state of the world, we hold out above the real an unbroken candle of blood and sleep beyond sleep.

What holds sway everywhere without being noticed: alchemies and their Jack-o'-lanterns.

The creator is pessimistic, the creation ambitious, therefore optimistic. The creature's rotation obeys their contrary orders.

Through loyalty, we learn never to be consoled.

Lacking the shore's support, do not trust yourself to the sea, but to the wind.

My birth gave me aggressive breathing.

One must salute the shadow with half-closed eyes. It leaves the orchard unplucked.

Suffering from the sickness of intuition.

The night rushes upon poetry, awakening breaks on it, when one is inspired to give it expression. Whatever the length of its headrope, poetry injures itself in us, and we in its fleeings.

It happens that our heart is as though driven out from our body. And our body is as though dead.

We do not attain the impossible, but it serves as a lamp for us. We will avoid the bee and the serpent, scorn the venom and the honey.

The flowering hawthorn was my first alphabet.

Comfort is crime, the spring in its rock told me.

Be consoled. Dying, you return everything you have been lent, your love, your friends. Until this living cold, gathered so many times.

The great ally of death, where it best conceals its gnats: memory. At the same time the persecutor of our odyssey, which lasts from a nightfall until the rose tomorrow.

Man, the air he breathes one day sucks him up; the earth takes what's left.

O too listless words, or words so slackly bound! Knucklebones scurrying in the decorous trickster's hand, I denounce you.

Killing has stripped me of my armour forever. You are my stripped armour forever. Which is right?

Who would dare to say that what we have destroyed was a hundred times more valuable than what we had unrelentingly dreamed and transfigured while whispering among the ruins?

No man, unless he is a living corpse, can feel the anchor in this life.

The history of man is the long succession of synonyms for the same vocable. To contradict this is a duty.

What was is no more. What was not must come into being. From the labyrinth with two entrances spring two hands full of passion. Lacking a spirit, what is it that inspires the livid, the atrocious or the blushing dispensatrix?

How could the end justify the means? There is no end, only means *ad perpetuum*, ever increasingly scheming.

Take away the breath of work, its inconceivable dynasty; return the free arts, should they cease to reflect everything, we would have the charnel-house.

The incalculable foulness of man *under* man, by destiny and preordination, could it have been dissolved by an enduring heart? Some, undefined, freeze or are ravaged on this hereditary gantry.

Whatever I plan out and undertake, I do not feel myself integral with neighboring death, or the risky and heightened liberty thrown down there, but with the harvests and the mirrors of our burning world.

Right to the end he had a genius for escaping; but it was in suffering that he escaped.

Suppress the concealed removal. The gods die only to be among us.

Lick his wound. The demons' ball opens to the sole musician.

To live, to be betrayed by life, to wish to live better and have power, all at the same time — that is infernal.

In this man were all the impatience and grimaces of the universe, and yet precisely the opposite. That lessened his bitterness, gave a treacherous savour to his hope which, thus estranged, did not reveal itself.

Misfortune is often rewarded with a greater affliction.

"I rebel and therefore throw out branches." Thus should men speak to the bonfire which tutors their rebellion.

Translations from René Char

When the sun commands, act little.

Like nature, when it proceeds to rebuild a mountain after our depre-
dations.

VENASQUE
Frosts in a mob are like you,
Men more passionate than the thicket;
The long winter winds are going to hang you.
The stone roof is the scaffold
Of an upright icy church.

The inclement distance is streaming and stationary. This is how a
proud look sees it.

If you don't accept what you are offered, one day you will be beggars
for even great refusals.

True clarity is discovered only at the foot of the stairs, in the door's
breathing.

Please dress me in tender snow, O skies, who oblige me to drink your
tears.

Grief is the last fruit — and immortal — of youth.

To set out on the path on one's own two feet, and, until evening, to
keep right on, getting to know it, treating it well, this path to which,
despite its vicious sand-traps, we show the straws of granted wishes
and the earth crossed with birds.

LATER UNCOLLECTED
POEMS AND TRANSLATIONS

The Tantramar Marsh near Jolicure. Coll. SHIRLEY MANN GIBSON

POEM

Frost walker,
bird of the crisp grass,
I make you a wintry field
from my body turned inside out:

not grain,
but the hidden blood,
oil of flight,
thick gruel of song.

The cold stubble
is a house
for the wingless,

but for you is the home
my strange sleep builds:

feed in my marrow,
nest in my entrails,
sing over my hard bones:
under the frozen flesh is shaping

the breaker of stone,
ploughman of black furrows.

OLD WOMAN

Old woman,
why do you comb your hair

against the rising sun,
your back to the sea,

nesting your face in the shadows
like a forgotten apple?

Your black comb
drops through the light:
a severed wing,

your honed arms
make a dancing rib-cage:

rhythm of the last fruit
before the frost,
gesture of bloodless vines.

Old woman,
what is it that you know

of the rising sun,
the sea at your back,

the darkness
into which you suddenly fall?

JOHN THOMPSON

POEM OF ABSENCE

An odour of moon, or
mown hay, green
cord wood,

the moon a yellow coat
in the mist;

the green glass of the wine bottle
does not yield
the body of things, nor

cut maple, grass, weave
of moon;

the wind pulls down the apples,
a coon squats
and gorges in the corn:

the open, where are you in
        the open?

RETORT

Song bears fruit
rooted deep in good earth:
apples of rich loam;

but this thundering
in blue space,
this orchard of wings!

JOHN THOMPSON

PIGEONS

You live against the wind,
forged birds breaking the cold;
you have gathered the stone
and iron of winter
into your hard grey bodies.

In the late afternoon, when the sun
is a dissolving jellied eye,
you shape your flight,
in threes and fours, a keen
metallic measure, cutting
dark curves in the light;

and when you fasten down
quiet with the depth of stone,
the taste of ripeness
and harvest hangs in the cold air;

but you are yourselves,
still, dark-feathered,
        gathering
what grain now from the glistening wind?

LISTENING

dark hands
and my birds dark

songs that may take you as
you turn away because
my sun suddenly

weighs is the edge
the burden
of a journey the edge

and I am everywhere turn
into my hands my
shining

there are birds there are
songs under
my dark hands
my shining

turn

I know why you have come so far

JOHN THOMPSON

POEM FOR RILKE

The moments of the heart are
slow: the opening
of the prodigal rose, the starry
stride of flamingos crossing
the white moon, the beast's gaze
into distances.

We are listening to the lyre
you touched: dark songs
grow from it and awaken us
into the world; we become
a breathing, an eye fleetingly
alive in the open; seized
by the dance, the fruits
of our body clap
like the wings of birds
entering the sun;

and as the song stills,
permitting our quiet
fall, the hand
of a god brushes the soil;

birds, we fold our wings
to discover the earth.

LIFE OUTFACED

I

Morning
puffy-eyed from a sleepless night
early morning no dawn headless morning
and this bituminous landscape stuck in orbit
dynamite blast in a drunken brain

men burrow deeper into their dark tunnels
day after day they shut themselves in their furnaces
and start again to flutter one eyelid then the other
to tack hour after hour right to the end
tack tack seeing nothing but the nightfall
into night's greedy paws

II

Mud tracks terrible tracks wolf tracks
those who don't know the rules ruin everything

those broken-faced great men loom up
clothed as always in an infernal cloud of ash
disconsolate haunters of the dark
from homes in charred craters
whose fires have lost their powers
fires without joy without flames fires without gods

drawn pumice faces
crumbling slate hands
faces like headstones where we break bread

JOHN THOMPSON

faces like peeling mirrors
reflecting nothing

III

Some shut themselves in silos
mingling with the last ears of grain
some store love's rebellion away in the loft

while others weld iron chains
and others prepare months of hatred

and once in a while a knife in the groin
and once in a while tell me you love me

IV

We must vigilantly keep our balance
between the vanished horizon and the imagined one
fearful of losing our foothold in the earth
of losing our sea legs
of no longer being able to walk the highwire
of no longer being able to walk on our hands

unhappy acrobats' sons
born in mid-air
in those memorable days when there were no nets

V

Vertigo seizes us by the waist and casts us down
we wind around stalks
while our hands spin the thin threads of hope
which will bind us to life

Later Uncollected Poems and Translations

ties ties of hope ties
Ariadne's delicate thread

VI

We must bed patience in like iron rails
take day by the hand and show it the way
which leads to men staggering on the shores of night

we have held this breath so long our faces grow strange
    wounds

life lived between walls takes on the mask of defeat
if in some crack there isn't a gleam of hope
the hope for love the hope for freedom
the hope that in time we will live all of us live
to love.

BEGINNING TO LIVE

The light knew just when to catch me —
at the pitch of my delirium
my eyes fixed in all the mirrors
my hands in the cataract's heart

I pushed aside
the dark palms I was offered
I left for good
those roads marked out with deadfires
for other wider roads
where my blood fused with the heavens
as an arrow with its target

I began to live.

GO ON LIVING

Thousands of junked images swarmed
over the thin film of those times
and we were haunted by visions
of a world we knew was in ruins

and cancer flourished invulnerable

and it wasn't fear but disgust
stuck in our throats

we felt like viruses
gaping wounds
pus poison wounds
rank blood and wounds
we felt like unclosed wounds
when certain words rose and went putrid
on our raw cracked lips

we felt guilty
heavy with guilt
for all the spilled blood crusted into scabs
for denatured animals for inanimate nature
for the days without bread for the dark times
and finally for life that has been stared down

we felt guilty
lost souls in a disaster

and to go on living
in our isolate silent cells
we began to invent a world
with the forms and colours
we had dreamed for it

ON THE OCCASION OF AN EXHIBITION

for David Silverberg

Against the weather and
    this eternal drift toward
"sanity"— death
    in fine clothes —

    we set
our dreams, our nakedness,
all the offences of our flesh and
the sweet barbarisms which
figure our nights:

beautiful women,
    and the animals,
who lie with us,

the eye and the line
    clean,
        the hand
unwavering.

Wife, mother, child, I loved her
for the world she made
from the night:

the clean tilt of the roof
straining north drawn
by the streaming stars;

coming into her great shade,
the sun blacked,
the cool
of her ground, a quietness
to lie with;

and inward the sun-webbed beams,
seething grasses,
the huge eyes lifting
through the fertile air;

this is her space now:
new stars lock
shingling her,

and in winter I feel her
homeward, looming,
a child calling
through the snow,

a lost child, cooed
to the breasts of the white bear.

Under this white shadow we have made
our home: salt, snow, hunger moon.
The whale's belly, the harpoons glisten.
We will die clean in our cold garden.
It is ours, we claim it: this sleep,
this waking with the white bears, the
ice, the gods.

TO THE POETS IN JAIL IN QUÉBEC

After all, the beer's cold:
what the fuck do I care
for taxi drivers or poets
in Quebec: prison
is a stupid word.

Mozart: the delicacy
seams the moment
Polski Ogörki
with what small love
we come together:

an Irishman laughs,
speaks as a boy
sweats and
moves like a wand.

Speak white. I love
my morning table, Wyatt
foolish, trying
to forge a suave pentameter,
whining
about rotten boughs.

After all the beer's cold
out of all this
beauty
something must come

the poet's words sing
in his cell,

JOHN THOMPSON

the sounding iron
rings in the blood.

Mozart. Snow. My table. Love
your broken arm

I want to say with those
poets in jail:
we will not be quiet,
who gives a fuck:
we will not be quiet.

WILLIAM BUTLER YEATS SURFACES
SOMEWHERE IN THE MARITIMES
COMPLETE WITH MYTHS, OR,
LEDA AND THE WHAT?

I seen where this feller come
all gotten up like
in a suit of feathers
sort of a big Canada Goose
with a fat orange beak shining like a lamp,
scattering down all over the place;

It were some dark,
old Charlie's eldest didn't know at all
what happened,
that beak nipping her neck and

lookit here boys through all those feathers he
done something,
a right big feller he were knew
a thing or two;

I seen where he
took off up acrosst the moon,
she yelled mad like
Charlie come out with
the twelve gauge couldn't see
nothing but wind clouds
of feathers shot up the night and

his eldest ain't been right since
goes around with a queer smile and a
loopy look in her eye picking feathers
out of her hair the shock
of it I imagine.

JOHN THOMPSON

TRANSLATIONS FROM
PAUL-MARIE LAPOINTE

SHORT STRAWS

I.

erosions: my flesh this fragile earth
plants

minerals compact of flower and fire

all geologies

2.

only when touched by death does the flower enter the girl
and in her frame its fragilities

she fearing the destruction of a town
burnt
its people and homes
the stone gardens

cruel season of death's menacing touch

3.

feast year
with a cry you press the weight of a kiss
the shattering of a star

4.

the gods in ambush
hidden among the rocks
falling like an apple from its tree
or spurting up — o geyser — and suddenly
in any epoch
past or to come
seizing us by the throat

earth's mystery

5.

the breathing of lovers
fills night's space
as a small sea shapes islands
in its sand
some small some large
for anguish or for abandon

6.

fly over me, asteroid

the mouth I love greets you from a spring where the fern
    demands obstinately to be loved all its life as a
    bouquet is loved and even more tenderly than being
    swept by seas and tears

7.

sea crystal
(I'm flying over it)
glass where warmth
and the wind's fluid hands swirl

it comes from the other end of the earth
keeping from continents and islands only light
and men and women moist from making love

8.

like rain
or passion
a tearful music possesses me

quick-tempered lover
jungle-mad chain-bound
whip-handler

more supple than the limbs of a woman making love
and like her piercing herself through and through

turning the whole world upside down

uttering cries

9.

in the clay the ancestral white lover
in the chalk the tender nets of her bones
in the plumage of a bird

a shimmering planet

10.

o dark distress

a tent of cries the archangel buckles under the burden of rains
this night swept by waves of terror

distress like a heart

my hip shaping the trajectory of a suffocated earth
I'm going to sleep in terror of alloys
shadowed by menacing

fuselaged speeds

11.

birth of the green
swathing everyone with rustling care
in her branches flare the heated passions
of whole families of suns

my taste of bark is no longer enough to contain my blood
nor my desire

summer's stiff tenderness

12.

I greet you
everyman's rain

like the advent of a fifth season

JOHN THOMPSON
244

13.

you can't tolerate this rhythm
this threatening terror
where the chicks scratch

concrete makes an altar to sacrifice to the gods
revolts, outrages

medusas are heaped up in the sun

15.

the teal utters a sun cry
a net to catch summer
a coop for the sea
                where girls will tan
                their salt-streaked legs

16.

for my sons I build wisdom
carnivorous architectures
there the families of their thoughts will make a home
raising angels animals

taming them
in the shattering of interstices
where beams join gathering light

the water of tears takes to distant interiors
ancient villages
the worthiest ancestors
and that divinity which from the beginning of time
               has never ceased to well up
between the stones

17.

under the spell of the lady of light
the saddened mallard takes flight

but then having entranced the lakes
she must disappear to the tropics
such is her fear of the snow

18.

as the rock its crystal vein
and the girl her arteries
so anguish polishes its ground

POEMS BECOME MOUNTAINS

The years are rags gone
in the wind; nothing
matters; O above
this frozen movie the stars go on
playing their marvellous games.

If we sit long enough
with this jar of black olives,
our cold table
will become a mountain,
olive trees, brine,
song.

all this talk, all
these silly fictions;

the sun settles and
gathers on us: nothing
grows;

voices dissolve, the ice
drifts dark on the tide;

sit down, sit down, replenish:

the blue air brings us birds.

Why do we think we are happy?

THE JUNIOR PROFESSOR'S REPLY

Your figure, love,
curves itself
into a man's memory
or to put it the way
a junior prof
at Mount Allison might
Helen with her thick
absconding limbs
about the waist
of Paris
did no better . . .
                    Irving Layton

O tempora, O mores
                    Horace

What wit, what wit:
O God, O Montreal, o toronto (lower case t)

I'm sad: as young Jim Joyce said
to Old Billyum "you're too old
for me to teach you anything"

I won't write stuff like that:
I write poems, not barroom anecdotes;
and as for the words I choose,
I do as I please;

I can take care of my women (thanks)
and of you: I'm waiting
down here in Jolicure, New Brunswick
with a feedbag full of dangerous poems.

Later Uncollected Poems and Translations
249

If you do come down,
leave behind your classy duds,
and that medallion you hang round your neck (you'll trip,
and the damn thing will strangle you)
and your hyperboles (you'll trip on those too):
plain talk, man, plain talk we want.

And if I'm not at home, look for me
in the Great Missaquash Bog
(bring a Chestnut Canoe, and a compass);
and for Christ's sake don't come flying in:
I'll gun you down for a black duck:
BANG! BANG! (both barrels)
you're dead.

PROFESSOR'S LAST STAND

Don't believe I'm here: I've packed,
gone without trace
somewhere north of north,

or I'm lying in the oily arms
of the richest woman in Calgary, Alberta;

don't you realise? I've been
disappearing all year:
at least half of me is eating
tea-dunked chappatis
outside Katmandu

and the other half is a fish,
brooding in the slow water
of Crooked Creek;

but if you still want to believe it,
O.K.; I guess there are a lot of words
half-words, syllables (etc) lying on the floor:

for Christ's sake don't pick them up, please
don't believe a word I've said.

A KIND OF NOTHING

for R.D.W.T.

There was a lady in France that, having had the small-pox, flayed the
skin off her face to make it more level; and whereas before she looked
like a nutmeg-grater, after she resembled an abortive hedge-hog.

Friend, I fear for you: too many
have jumped off already; why
fly around like a mad moth, loon, bat,
crazy owl (walking naked, indeed!)

when you could lie warm
and furry in an old box, sip cream and
feel fat with nine lives; as safe
as a toad in God's pocket!

But you've gone too far: the worm
is under your nail; already cock-eyed,
God knows what you'll be seeing: in your garden
that thing with a rake,
on your poor bones, fantastical
puff-paste.

What would you do,
digging up Old Nick's dirt?

But what's the use; you'll persist
in this damned profession; and maybe

we can fall into the same dark water together,
build a floating world, laugh,

laugh more, spend lusciously
at least half a life, then
take to the woods and sleep like angels
on a pillow stuffed with a litter of porcupine quills.

What do you say, familiar,
friend?

LEFT-HANDED EPITHALAMION

for Bruce and Linda

Li Po threw poems into the river;
I have preserved this,
a small, bent celebration:

honest wine, fat animals, sweet corn, marvellous
potatoes,

your own hands fierce and
tender as wild strawberries.

It is difficult to speak of the beauty I would wish.

What is a poem anyway that you ask for it
on a day when the apples grow fat without me,

and the gods are here and have spoken
(I know they have their price)

and then poets are dangerous: their words
menace the perfect garden.

Just now, Apollo stopped me. (Look,
his light is still in the grass)

he told me simply, "serve me"; I won't argue.

But one last word, your own, call it love;

then, leave poets out of it,
they have only poor things to say:

ah! ladies, gentlemen, gentle lady, gentle man,
this day is yours.

JOHN THOMPSON

[GHAZAL XXXIX]

I am dark
I'll wash my own hands.

All the bad fighting, people
in bad brew;

I'll have to die: no one's
worth it.

Lord: *(three words unclear)*
sit *(one word unclear)*

I'll *(one word unclear)*
with you

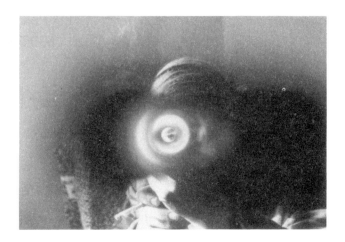

John Thompson looking down the barrel of his
pump-action shotgun, winter, 1974. Coll. SHIRLEY MANN GIBSON

NOTES ON THE POEMS

MAIN SOURCES

I have derived the texts of Thompson's poems and compiled the following notes on them, unless otherwise indicated, from the following sources:

(1) John Thompson, *At the Edge of the Chopping There Are No Secrets* (Toronto: Anansi, 1973), referred to in the notes as *At the Edge*.

(2) John Thompson, *Stilt Jack* (Toronto: Anansi, 1978).

(3) John Thompson, *I Dream Myself into Being: Collected Poems*, introduced by James Polk (Toronto: Anansi, 1991).

(4) John Thompson, *Translations from René Char's* La Parole en Archipel *and Other Works* (PhD thesis, Michigan State University, 1966).

(5) Final drafts, working drafts and notes in typescript or manuscript prepared by Thompson, together with other material and documentation either written by him or associated with him, owned by Shirley Mann Gibson.

(6) Thompson's "black book," referred to as *BB* in the following notes: a black, cloth-bound sketch book measuring approximately 12 x 15 inches, unruled, containing working and final drafts of poems and some additional material. Its first entry is dated September 22, 1970; the last is dated October 18, 1975. Thompson had a fitted leather satchel made by Sackville Harness Ltd. to case this book. Both are owned by Gibson.

(7) Cassette tape of a reading Thompson gave at the University of New Brunswick in spring, 1974, designated as *Tape*.

(8) Peter Sanger, *Sea Run: Notes on John Thompson's Stilt Jack* (Antigonish, NS: Xavier Press [*Antigonish Review*], 1986), referred to as *SR*.

PART I: Books

AT THE EDGE OF THE CHOPPING
THERE ARE NO SECRETS

The editing of *At the Edge of the Chopping There Are No Secrets* was carried out by Margaret Atwood. She met with Thompson in Sackville. Among Atwood's editorial notes for Anansi are these words: "He's very easy to work with. . . . The arrangement is basically mine, as he had no suggestions other than alphabetical order. It follows loosely the kind of arrangement suggested by Jim [Polk]. The logic moves from the initial 'wife' group through some lush 'thing' and 'scene' poems, through some sparer 'Crow' poems, into a 'winter' and 'hunger' group; then through the dream, axe and murder poems through some 'return' poems to a final kind of 'realization' poem, rounding off with another 'wife' poem that connects with the first one . . . . Edited out a few . . . got some of the Early Yeats lines and phrases out. I think the finished version is pretty fine."

Dated drafts exist for only ten of the poems in *At the Edge*. The Jolicure fire probably destroyed drafts preceding Thompson's first use of *BB* in September, 1970. The earliest published of the *At the Edge* poems was "Cold Wind," which appeared in *The Dalhousie Review* in 1967. Eleven more poems which do not appear in *BB* were published in various Canadian periodicals between January and December, 1970.

Household
The line ends were determined by Anansi.

Our Arcs Touch
In *BB* dated September 22, 1970. It is the first entry. See Section 26 of Yeats's "Estrangement: Extracts from a Diary kept in 1909": "We are, as seen from life, an artifice, an emphasis, an uncompleted arc perhaps. Those whom it is our business to cherish and celebrate are complete arcs."

Fish
Thompson wrote on the final publisher's draft, "note: punctuate as is."

Horse
In *Tape*, Thompson self-deprecatingly calls "Horse" a "small rural apocalypse" (see the Revelation of St. John, particularly chapters 6 and 7). But, as Thompson says, he also saw a horse in a field.

Barn

In *BB* dated December 7-10, 1970, and titled "Barn I." Its companion, "Barn II" (see pp. 236 and 272), was cut from *At the Edge*. In *Tape*, Thompson explains that the barn was one at his Wood Point home.

Scene

In *BB* dated December 4, 1970. In *Tape*, Thompson calls this poem "a kind of exercise" and explains it is based on a postcard reproducing part of a medieval pictorial calendar.

Black Smith Shop

The original typescript contains a second stanza which was cut during editing:

> and I feel my words poor as I speak them,
> coming out into the sun,
> falling, broken stones;

Turnip Field

In *Tape*, Thompson says of the man, "he's doing his job," and emphasizes the distance between the observing poet and this self-absorbed, narrowly intent figure.

Colville's Crow

In *Tape*, Thompson tells the story upon which the poem is based — of Alex Colville's keeping a dead crow in the refrigerator to use as a model for a painting. The poem is "meant to be slightly witty."

Crow and Rabbit

In *Tape*, Thompson notes that he was trying "simply to present something in the world without comment." He cites William Carlos Williams as an exemplar.

January February March Et Cetera

In *Tape*, Thompson comments, "There's a steal from Yeats in there — 'crazy salads'." See Yeats's "A Prayer for My Daughter."

The Supermarket Invaded

In *BB* dated February 6, 1971, where "slovenly" in the third line reads "unshapely."

Return

In *BB* dated October 18, 1970.

"Winter Is by far the Oldest Season"
This title first appeared on the top line of the first page of *BB* like an epigraph for the whole book of drafts. A source is Gaston Bachelard, *The Poetics of Space*, translated by Maria Jolas (New York: Orion, 1964), 41. Thompson may have made his own translation from *La Poétique de l'espace* (1958). In *BB* the poem was worked out in December, 1970, and on January 17 and 23, 1971.

The Skins of a Dream
The "wine-dark" of stanza five perhaps comes most immediately from Part VIII of Yeats's "A Woman Young and Old."

Down Below
In the last stanza, "a candle burned" evokes both Char and Hopkins. See the second paragraph of Thompson's translation of Char's "The Brittle Age" (p. 217). Roy Snowdon, who lived in Wood Point, was Thompson's mentor in the woods and on the water.

The Narrow Road
In *BB* dated March 19, 1972. In *Tape,* Thompson explains that the title is one "which I stole" from Basho.

Moving Out, Moving In
In *BB* dated October 31, 1971. R.G.E. is the poet R.G. Everson, whose Montreal and Florida addresses appear elsewhere in *BB*. The poem was originally subtitled "The Man Who Loves Geography." Stanza six plays with Wallace Stevens's "The Emperor of Ice-Cream." Thompson's poem also draws upon Bachelard's *The Poetics of Space.*

Burnt Coat Head
In *BB* dated October 6, 1970. It was written after a visit to Burnt Coat Head on the Bay of Fundy Noel shore, East Hants County, Nova Scotia — a famous shorebird- and hawk-haunted place. The last stanza contains an allusion to Dylan Thomas's "Over St. John's Hill."

Picasso: *La Jeune Fille sur la Boule*; Lascaux: *Stag Frieze*
In *Tape,* Thompson notes that he had reproductions of these two paintings stuck on the wall above his desk. Char's sequence "Lascaux" (pp. 174-175) must also have been in his mind.

Norman Tower's
Thompson's Wood Point farmhouse was owned by the Tower family.

Norman Tower, the occupant previous to the Thompsons, committed suicide after learning he was terminally ill.

On the Tolar Canal

The Anansi editors and typesetter had to adjust the lineation of the first two lines of this poem into four lines. Thompson ended line 1 at "Lakes," line 2 at "burning."

Ewe's Skull on the Aboideau at Carter's Brook

In *Tape*, Thompson describes driving from Wood Point to Sackville every day and seeing this skull as he crossed Carter's Brook. He mentions that Charles G.D. Roberts "lived just down the road from the brook."

The Brim of the Well

The first lines derive from Bachelard's *The Poetics of Space*, chapter 4, "Nests."

The Bread Hot From the Oven

A fragment in *BB* suggests a probable date of February, 1971.

STILT JACK

Dedication

The text was stipulated in Clause 6 of Thompson's will.

Epigraphs

The first comes from Yeats's "High Talk." The second is slightly misquoted from Stickney's "Mt. Lykaion." The third is a conflation of a phrase from Psalm 121 and one of Emily Dickinson's letters. See *SR*. In one typescript Thompson wrote instead of epigraph three: "Emily Dickinson (from the Letters)?????" On the final typescript given to Douglas Lochhead, Thompson scribbled the present wording of epigraph three in a distraught hand.

Ghazals

An earlier, undated version of this introduction appears in one of the typescripts Thompson circulated among friends. It reads:

Notes on the Ghazal

These poems are based on a traditional Urdu form — the ghazal — which has its roots in very early Arabic poetry. By tradition, they are first of all love poems and explore the subtleties of complex relationships in much the same way as the Italian and Shakespearean sonnet sequences. The most powerfully felt and expressed emotions, however, are those associated with sadness, melancholy, loss, despair, grief. The atmosphere of sadness and grief that pervades the ghazal is perfectly epitomized in the fact that the word "ghazal" means the agonized cry of the gazelle when it is cornered after the chase and realizes that the game is up. In English I think the late dark sonnets of Shakespeare and some of Donne's Holy Sonnets come, in their different ways, close to this mood.

So much for "content." As to structure, there are no close parallels in English. And the structure of the ghazal, which is its essence, is what is most likely to give the English reader — accustomed to "closed," narrative, continuous, logical poems — some trouble. Essentially, each "couplet" of the ghazal may be considered a poem in itself. From couplet to couplet one must literally leap without expecting what we normally think of as "sense," especially continuous sense. If the poems, and the sequence, hold together, it is because of undercurrents of mood, tone, feeling, attitude, cumulative imagery, etc.

In my own ghazals I have been pulling stunts both within the couplet, and the line: an extension of the principle outlined above. I hope they don't prove too much of a bloody puzzlement and that some of all this helps. I've been working in the dark with the poems — but why not?

Translations of the Urdu ghazal here appeared in magazines and in book form in the USA, particularly the work of the brilliant 19th century poet Ghalib. And some Americans have picked up the form as their own, most notably Adrienne Rich. The attraction for me, and I suspect for others, is that both the atmosphere and the structural nature of the ghazal seem tuned to the modern sensibility.

Thompson wrote at the top of the page from which this text is transcribed the alternative title, "Tarantella." Both the introduction to *Stilt Jack* and the rejected draft show some similarities to Jim Harrison's introduction to his ghazals in *Outlyer and Ghazals* (New York: Simon and Schuster, 1971).

Ghazal I

In *BB* dated September 23, 1973. Titled "Setting the Chimney Stone: A Ghazal," it is inscribed "for Wayne." R.D. Wayne Tompkins, a poet and former Mount Allison colleague of Thompson's, left

Mount Allison in the summer of 1974. In a letter to me, Tompkins explained that he and Thompson discovered the ghazal form in two Norton anthologies of poetry in the late summer and early fall of 1973. Many of Thompson's early ghazals are part of a poetic dialogue between Tompkins and Thompson. In an undated note, probably sent in the fall of 1973, Thompson wrote: "Wayne: Since my series is turning into (among other thing) a dialogue with WBY I'm going to use the Malachi Stilt Jack poem as title or epigraph. I hereby lay claim to this." In *Tape*, before starting to read ghazals I-XI (omitting II), Thompson says, "there are a lot of steals in these too — in some ways a dialogue with Yeats and some others, too."

Ghazal II

In *BB* dated September 23, 1973. Titled "Shall These Bones Live" in some typescripts.

Ghazal III

In *BB* dated September 25, 1973, and subtitled "for Wayne: it's my turn."

Ghazal IV

In *BB* dated September 29, 1973, and titled "Another Ghazal."

Ghazal V

In *BB* dated September 29, 1973. In some typescripts this ghazal and the following one are titled "Two Poems."

Ghazal VI

In *BB* dated September 30, 1973. There, line 6 reads: "dies with the wind; birds roost, waking claws shine."

Ghazal VII

In *BB* dated October 2, 1973, and dedicated "for D.G.J." — that is, D.G. Jones. My annotation of "Albany" in line 2 in *SR* was wrong. The reference is to the treatment Roethke received at Albany General Hospital after a manic breakdown in 1946. See Allan Seager, *The Glass House: The Life of Theodore Roethke* (New York: McGraw-Hill, 1968). In couplet seven, "is this my table?" is a wry joke. But see "on my table" in ghazal IV; "Perfection of tables" in XXXVII; "Thou shalt prepare a table before me," Psalm 23; "the table of my memory" in *Hamlet*, I: 5; "Thy beauty's form in table of my heart" in Shakespeare's Sonnet XXIV and "Thy gift, thy tables are within my brain / Full charactered with lasting memory" in Sonnet XXII. There are more.

See *SR*. On the back of the page upon which this ghazal is drafted, Thompson wrote, "everything's emptying out: my wife's gone."

Ghazal VIII

In *BB* dated October 2, 1973. An uncancelled couplet in *BB*, coming after couplet four, reads: "Perched on the beaver dam, I'm happy. / Jenny takes ten trout. Beaver work by our hooks." Thompson underlined the "it" in the ghazal's last line, confirming its relationship to "face." He reads with the same emphasis in *Tape*.

Ghazal IX

In *BB* this ghazal was worked out on October 11 and (mainly) October 16, 1973. As the Toronto poet Martin Singleton pointed out to me, couplet five derives from an Isley Brothers song popular in the early 1970s. The second line of couplet eight ends, " . . . game; we forgot my soldering iron" in *BB*. On his final typescript, Thompson wrote of the "number nine" in couplet two: "Must correspond with number of the ghazal if the order is changed." In the *BB* version, the following two couplets appear after couplet three:

> The ferret rides first class in the sack, earns it by blood work
> in the dark; stays clean; homes in the night bag. Who's fed?

> The dog, the rat's rich soon dead;
> coin bangs in the catcher's palm.

Thompson circled these couplets and wrote "revise" opposite them.

Ghazal X

In *BB* dated October 4, 1973.

Ghazal XI

In *BB* dated October 12-13, 1973. The seventeenth century spelling "flie" in couplet six alludes to John Donne and Isaac Walton. See also Emily Dickinson's poem "I heard a fly buzz — when I died".

Ghazal XII

In *BB* dated October 19 and October 22, 1973. In the original draft, "after Tu Fu" does not appear.

Ghazal XIII

In *BB* dated October 24, 1973. In his final typescript, in the second line of couplet two, Thompson used the proofreading code of a triple line under the capital "H" of "He's"; he wanted the point clear. See the last couplet.

Ghazal XIV

In *BB* placed and dated "Ottawa, 3 December '73." In *BB* the ghazal is inscribed "for René Char." The last couplet derives from Char's *Partage Formel*. Part of the imagery of the ghazal is also adapted from Thompson's translation of Char's "Needle Mirage." In the *BB* version, couplet three reads: "Bread of heaven. Mortal strife. / Plunge from the two. In close." This ghazal celebrates the beginning of Thompson's relationship with Shirley Mann Gibson.

Ghazal XV

In *BB* dated January, 1974. The *BB* version gives "fruit" for "flower" in couplet two; inserts "woman?" at the end of couplet five; and concludes after "will you" in the last couplet with the words, "keep me forever in a warm forest?"

Ghazal XVI

In *BB* the last couplet of ghazal XVI is drafted and dated November 24, 1973. It is followed by the partially cancelled couplet: "I'm too young to write love poems; where's the moon? / I threw myself to the dogs: they wouldn't eat." The rest of ghazal XVI appears in *BB* dated January 26, 1974. "Tobin" in couplet four is the name of the maker of Thompson's double-barrelled shotgun. This gun was not, as some have said, buried with him. It was confiscated by the Sackville Police Department, acting under court order, before Thompson's death.

Ghazal XVII

In *BB* dated Sunday, Jolicure, January 27. The year must have been 1974. Couplet two quotes the dying Keats. The note in *SR* explaining "Page" is wrong. The Page in question is likely a baseball player, the great pitcher Satchell Paige; I suspect Thompson misspelled his name. In BB and in all other texts of the ghazal except Thompson's final typescript, "Csonka" appears instead of "Page." Larry Csonka, born in 1946, was a running back with the Miami Dolphins. In the final typescript, the change to "Page" is made in Thompson's hand. The archaic spelling of "teares" in couplet five is consistent in all texts.

Ghazal XVIII

In *BB*, but not dated. It comes after two pages of erratic and sometimes completely illegible notes, drafts and scattered phrases. One of these pages is dated January 27, 1974. This is one of many of the ghazals which recall passages in Gaston Bachelard's *La Psychoanalyse* du Feu (1938), translated as *The Psychoanalysis of Fire* (Boston: Beacon,

1964). Herbert Burke told me that Thompson carefully read Bachelard's book in the Beacon Press edition throughout the writing of *Stilt Jack*. The book's preface is by Northrop Frye.

Ghazal XIX

In *BB*, but not dated. This ghazal was not in Thompson's final typescript.

Ghazal XX

Not in *BB*. This ghazal appears in Thompson's final typescript. I believe it was written in the middle spring of 1974. "Meton" in couplet five is a character in Walter Savage Landor's novel *Pericles and Aspasia* (1856), to which Thompson had probably been led by Yeats's poem "To a Young Beauty."

Ghazal XXI

In *BB*, dated May 9, 1974. In couplet three, the word "speck" appears in the place of "thread." Thompson cancelled "speck."

Ghazal XXII

In *BB*, where Thompson has scribbled "date?" at the top of the page.

Ghazal XXIII

In *BB*, but not dated, except for some minor revisions which are dated March 3, 1975. It was probably written in May or June, 1974.

Ghazal XXIV

In *BB*, dated "June ? 74" in Thompson's hand.

Ghazal XXV

In *BB*, dated August 13, 1974.

Ghazal XXVI

In *BB*, dated September 24, 1974. In couplet three, "smell" was originally "scent."

Ghazal XXVII

Not in *BB*.

Ghazal XXVIII

Not in *BB*. In the final typescript, the first line of the last couplet reads: "the white whale, John Thompson, in her face." Thompson cancelled his name by striking it through and printing "STILT JACK" in its place. The poet's naming himself was among the formal traditions of the Urdu ghazal. Couplet five draws upon a song by Carly Simon.

Ghazal XXIX

In *BB*, dated October 12 and 13, 1974.

Ghazal XXX

In *BB*, dated October 13, 1974.

Ghazal XXXI

In *BB*, dated October 18, 1975. "Strait" in line 7 appears in all versions. See the play of "straight, strait" in Ghazal XXVIII and Donne's "Hymne to God My God, In My Sickness". The capital "T" of "Thine" in the last line is underlined three times. Thompson wrote at the bottom of the *BB* page: "For David, Nancy, Linda, Bill."

Ghazal XXXII

Not in *BB*. No date.

Ghazal XXXIII

Not in *BB*. No date.

Ghazal XXXIV

Not in *BB*. No date. The poet Robert Bringhurst pointed out to me that proper names in couplets 2, 3 and 4 refer not only to mountains in the Himalayas and the Swiss Alps but also to makers of mountaineering equipment (Chouinard, Karrimor, Stubai, Vasque) and to the equipment itself (Kernmantel is a type of climbing rope; a Jumar is a sliding rope clamp). Bringhurst suspects that Bonnaiti is a typographical error and that the reference is to Walter Bonatti, a famous solo climber and mountaineering author.

Ghazal XXXV

Not in *BB*. But among the manuscript drafts are worksheets for this ghazal which indicate that Thompson was working on it in March, 1974. The translation was the consequence of a correspondence with a friend, probably by then a professor, at Michigan State whose first name was Surjit but whose last name I cannot either decipher or recover through enquiries. Thompson must have asked him for help in researching the history of the ghazal in Urdu poetry. In a letter of reply, Surjit recommended D.J. Matthews and C. Shackle, *An Anthology of Classical Urdu Love Lyrics: Text and Translations* (London: Oxford University Press, 1972). A photocopy of the Introduction to this book survives among Thompson's papers. He also read another recommended book, Ahmed Ali, *The Golden Tradition: An Anthology of Urdu Poetry* (New York: Columbia University Press, 1973), and made notes on Chapter II, "The Anguished Heart: Mir and the Eighteenth Century." Several of the passages in this chapter Thompson copied whole. A draft title page in Thompson's hand indicates that he considered translating fifty of Mir's ghazals. What became ghazal XXXV may have been the only fruit of a proposed collaboration with Surjit. In the drafts of ghazal XXXV, Thompson's reworking of a literal English translation his friend seems to have sent him moves away from faded diction and vague phrasing into this ghazal.

Ghazal XXXVI

Written on an envelope loosely inserted in *BB* and dated December 12, 1975. Before Thompson cancelled the extra words, couplet one read: "don't know what a poem is. / I am struck by an arrow." The capitalization in the last two couplets is, at certain points, inconsistent with the use of capitals in the rest of the ghazal and elsewhere in the Anansi texts, but all three printings are faithful to Thompson's manuscript.

Ghazal XXXVII

In *BB*, dated November 5, 1974. It is headed "Last Poem." Beside that heading, written in a different-coloured ink in a more erratic hand, is "XXXVIII." That scribbled number may explain why the First Encounter publication of the next ghazal (Vol.7, 1975-1977) numbered it as XXXIX. This ghazal refers, among many other things (see *SR*), to the burning down of the Jolicure house on September 25, 1974.

Ghazal XXXVIII

Not in *BB*. This ghazal exists in a manuscript version and in a typed transcription made by Douglas Lochhead with the note, "Written April 22, 1976. D.G.L." The manuscript is headed "XXXVIII" followed by an exclamation mark, both in Thompson's hand. At the bottom of it, Thompson wrote: "Holograph of the last poem for *Stilt Jack* Point de Bute, just after Easter 1976 For Ross who is mentioned — With love (Hold this I don't have a fucking copy)." "Ross" is Ross Galbraith.

PART TWO: Uncollected Poems and Translations

EARLY UNCOLLECTED POEMS AND TRANSLATIONS

[*La Cloche qui Sonne*]
    Michigan's Voices 2(1), 1961: 21. A prosaic English version might read:
    "The bell which rings / its dying / moments / catches me on an eternal
    / point / of worlds which have never existed; / burning / I sense / the
    impenetrable / eyes / of death."

The Dead Lost on the Eiger
    Tarot: A Magazine of the Arts 1:2 (1961): 29.

The Drunken Boat
    Tarot: A Magazine of the Arts 2:1 (1962): 22-24. The ellipsis in stanza
    16 is Rimbaud's; that in stanza 17 is Thompson's;.

The Man in the Wind
    Michigan's Voices 2:3 (Spring 1962): 1; *Tarot: A Magazine of the Arts* 2:1
    (1962): 25-26; G.J. Firmage, ed., *A Garland for Dylan Thomas* (New
    York: Clarke & Way, 1963): 126-127.

A Tale of the Moon
    Tarot: A Magazine of the Arts 2:1 (1962): 61-62. The centred the lines
    may show the influence of Dylan Thomas.

A Fever on the River
    Tarot: A Magazine of the Arts 2:1 (1962): 63-64.

Incantation for a New Season
    Michigan's Voices 3:2 (Spring 1963): 3.

Venus Anadyomene
    Michigan's Voices 3:3 (Summer 1963): 25.

Poem on Two Paintings of Van Gogh
    Red Cedar Review 2:1 (Spring 1964): 20.

TRANSLATIONS FROM RENÉ CHAR

The source used for the text is John Thompson, *Translations from René Char's*
La Parole en Archipel *and Other Works with an Introductory Essay* (PhD thesis,
Michigan State University, 1966). Char's texts appear opposite the trans-

lations in Thompson's thesis. There are some differences between these texts and those in René Char, *Oeuvres Complètes* (Paris: NRF Gallimard, 1983). In *Oeuvres Complètes*, Char eliminated Part I of "À Deux Enfants" (translated by Thompson as Part I of "To Two Children"); made "Epitaphe" (Thompson's "Epitaph") Part II of "L'arbre Frappé" (Thompson's "The Struck Tree"); changed the title of "La Soif Hospitalière" printed "Venasque" (Thompson uses the same title) from the sequence "L'Age Cassant" (Thompson's "The Brittle Age") as a separate poem.

René Char (1907-1988) was born in the freshwater fishing village of L' Isle-sur-la-Sorgue, not far from Avignon, in Provence. He was a prominent member of the surrealist movement during the early 1930s. His first major collection, *Le Marteau sans Maître*, appeared in 1934. Between its publication and the outbreak of the Second World War, he gradually distanced himself from surrealist activities, affirming his rootedness in the landscape and poetic traditions of Provence and developing a code of obdurate, intuitive humanism to counter the egocentric nihilism and autocratic manipulation which had become increasingly evident in surrealist circles. When hostilities began, he fought initially in an artillery unit and later as part of a rear guard delaying the German advance and protecting retreating French army personnel and civilians. Upon the fall of France in 1940, he returned to L'Isle-sur-la-Sorgue, but was forced to go into hiding to escape execution by the Vichy government. Between January 1941 and 1945, under the pseudonym Captain Alexandre, he directed sections of the French Resistance in the Provence region. He kept a notebook of observations and lyrical aphorisms during this period which became *Feuillets d'Hypnos*, published by Gallimard at the insistence of Char's friend, Albert Camus, in 1946. This book is one of the finest to have been written during the war. It was republished as part of *Fureur et Mystère* in 1948. That collection established Char's international reputation. Among other artists, Kandinsky, Matisse, Picasso, Giacometti, Braque and Miró illustrated his work. In 1955, Pierre Boulez set to music three of the poems of *Le Marteau sans Maître*. Paul Celan's German translations of some of Char's poems appeared in 1959. Char was a close friend of Braque, Georges Bataille and Heidegger (whom he was instrumental in inviting to give three seminars in Provence between 1966 and 1969). Pierre Reverdy addressed Char in "Vous Êtes Vous Aussi . . ." (in my translation) as:

Dear Char, searcher for
    dense stones beneath the earth
    who knows how to bring them to sunlight

JOHN THOMPSON

to make words from them
of the purest matter.

In "To a Dog Injured in the Street," a poem in *The Desert Music and Other Poems* (1954), William Carlos Williams wrote:

René Char
> you are a poet who believes
> in the power of beauty
> to right all wrongs.
> I believe it also.

A special issue of the Montreal review *Liberté*, titled "Hommage à René Char," was published in July-August, 1968. Thompson was familiar with the first major English translation of a substantial body of Char's work, *Hypnos Waking* (New York: Random House, 1956). He conceived his thesis as a sequel to it, translating work published by Char between 1950 and 1962 which had not appeared in that collection. In a letter to Gibson dated October 5, 1973, Thompson wrote, "It still seems to me that there is a book, and a very beautiful book, to be had from these translations."

LATER UNCOLLECTED POEMS AND TRANSLATIONS

Poem
> *Fiddlehead* 71 (Spring 1967): 59.

Old Woman
> *Fiddlehead* 71 (Spring 1967): 58.

Poem of Absence
> Cut from *At the Edge*. This and the following three poems exist only in undated typescripts. It seems safe to assume they were written before the first entry in *BB* which is dated September, 1970. Stylistically, the four poems resemble the two preceding ones. I believe they were all written between 1966 and 1968.

Retort
> Cut from *At the Edge*.

Pigeons
> Cut from *At the Edge*.

Listening
Cut from *At the Edge*.

Poem for Rilke
Cut from *At the Edge*. This poem exists only in undated typescripts. Its style and the fact that it was among a group of Thompson's poems broadcast on CBC *Anthology* in 1970 lead me to think it was written in 1968 or 1969.

Translations From Roland Giguère
Thompson's translations are taken from *Ellipse* 2 (1970): 11-15, 17, 21. Giguère's texts appear in *L'Âge de la Parole: Poèmes 1949-1960* (Ottawa: Éditions de l'Hexagone, 1965) under the titles "La Vie Dévisagée," "Continuer à Vivre" and "Vivre Mieux."

On the Occasion of an Exhibition
In *BB*, dated December 3, 1970. Published in *First Encounter* 4 (1971-1972): 77.

Barn II
In *BB*, dated December 7, 1970. Published in *First Encounter* 4 (1971-1972): 79.

Arctic
White Pelican (Fall 1971): 3. "Arctic" was in the typescript of *At the Edge*, but Thompson agreed to cut it because it did not fit the collection. A silkscreen print of this poem was made by David Silverberg, a professor of fine arts at Mount Allison, and copies of it were distributed in Sackville in 1970 as part of an ecology publicity campaign. Lineation in *White Pelican*, Silverberg's print and Thompson's typescript varies. Thompson gave Alan Bishop a handwritten copy of this poem in the winter of 1970.

To the Poets in Jail in Québec
In *BB* dated "last day of February, 1971." This is the only rough draft poem of sufficient finish in *BB* to justify retrieval. No typescript of it seems to exist. At its finest, it foreshadows *Stilt Jack*. In the second stanza, "Polski Ogörki" are garlic dill pickles.

William Butler Yeats Surfaces Somewhere in the Maritimes . . .
First Encounter 4 (1971-1972): 80. I have found no typescript or manuscript of this poem.

Short Straws: Translations from Paul-Marie Lapointe
These translations are taken from *Ellipse* 1 (1972): 37-45. Lapointe's texts appear in *Le Réel Absolu: Poèmes 1948-1963* (Ottawa: Éditions de l'Hexagone, 1971) under the sequence title "Courtes Pailles." Number 14 is omitted in both the French and the English texts printed in *Ellipse.*

Poems Become Mountains
In *BB*, dated January 23, 1973. Published in *First Encounter* 5 (1973-1974): 40.

Hilda & Reshard
Unpublished. Manuscript page headed "Wood Point 31 March 73." The poem is addressed to Hilda Woolner and the novelist and poet Reshard Gool. It is signed "John."

The Junior Professor's Reply
In *BB* undated, but probably written in the late fall of 1973. A typescript also exists. Thompson reads the poem in *Tape*. He begins by saying, "I understand there's a poet called Irving Layton." He reads from the passage of Layton used as one of the epigraphs (from Layton's "The Lambs Are All Around Us") and adds, "I thought it was about bloody time that a reply was written." Layton published his poem in 1954.

Professor's Last Stand
In typescript. Thompson read this in *Tape*, commenting, "It's about standing up before a class wondering what the hell you're doing there." The second stanza probably plays with the possibility that Thompson might have taken a university position in Calgary in 1966.

A Kind of Nothing
First Encounter 6 (1974-1975): 45. Thompson read this in *Tape*, noting that the poem's epigraph is taken from John Webster's *The Duchess of Malfi*, as are several of the poem's phrases (II:1; V:5; IV:2). The poem is dedicated to Wayne Tompkins. In *Tape*, Thompson mentions that he wrote the poem for someone who was "giving up studying of certain recondite matters in Milton to write poetry, which strikes me as a damned crazy thing to do."

Left-Handed Epithalamion
Several typescripts but no manuscript of this exist. It probably was written in 1974.

[Ghazal XXXIX]

Thompson was in the Tantramarsh Club in Sackville with Akis Patapiou and Jon Wright, two of his students, on April 23, 1976. He wrote this poem (untitled), threw it on the floor and ground it with his boot. Akis Patapiou retrieved the poem later. I have worked with a photocopy of the original and with Akis Patapiou's transcription which reads:

> I am dark
> I'll wash my own hands.
>
> All the bad fighting, people
> in bad brew;
>
> I'll have to die! no one's
> worth it.
>
> Lord, buy me a
> drink
>
> I'll die
> with grief.

My truncated text represents as much as can be deciphered with reasonable certainty. I would tentatively transcribe the full poem as follows:

> I am dark
> I'll wash my own hands.
>
> All the bad fighting, people
> in bad brew;
>
> I'll have to die: no-one's
> worth it.
>
> Lord: born to man
> sit down
>
> I'll drink:
> with you.

This attempt may have the merit of showing that there can be no definite full text of ghazal XXXIX. The original is signed in a hand which has disintegrated into wild, sprawling scrawls: "John Thompson, The End."

BIBLIOGRAPHY

SELECTED PRIMARY SOURCES

Final drafts, working drafts and notes in typescript or manuscript made by Thompson, together with other miscellaneous material and documentation. Owned by Shirley Mann Gibson.

Thompson's "black book," a black, cloth-bound sketch book measuring 12 x 15 inches, unruled, containing handwritten working and final drafts of poems. Its first entry is dated September 22, 1970, and the last is dated October 18, 1975. Owned by Shirley Mann Gibson.

Cassette tape of a reading Thompson gave at the University of New Brunswick in spring, 1974. Original and copies are in the possession of Shirley Mann Gibson.

Thompson, J. *Translations from René Char's* La Parole en Archipel *and Other Works*. PhD thesis, Michigan State University, 1966.

Thompson, J. *At the Edge of the Chopping There Are No Secrets*. Toronto: Anansi, 1973.

Thompson, J. *Stilt Jack*. Toronto: Anansi, 1978.

Thompson, J. *I Dream Myself into Being: Collected Poems*. Introduced by James Polk. Toronto: Anansi, 1991.

SELECTED SECONDARY SOURCES

Ali, A., ed. and trans. *The Golden Tradition: An Anthology of Urdu Poetry*. New York: Columbia University Press, 1973.

Atwood, M. "Before." In *Interlunar*. Toronto: Oxford University Press, 1984.

Atwood, M. "Last Testaments: Pat Lowther and John Thompson,." In *Second Words: Selected Critical Prose*. Toronto: Anansi, 1982.

Bachelard, G. *The Psychoanalysis of Fire*. Translated by A.C.M. Ross. Boston: Beacon, 1964.

Barbour, D. "John Thompson." In *Canadian Writers Since 1960: Second Series*. Vol. 60, Dictionary of Literary Biography. Detroit: Gale, 1987.

Barbour, D. "*Late Work at the Kitchen Table*: Phyllis Webb's Water and Light." *West. Coast. Line.* 6 (Winter 1991-1992): 103-117.

Bell, W. *Mountains Beneath the Horizon*. London: Faber and Faber, 1950.

Bemrose, J. "No Sense But a Lot of Feeling." *Toronto Star*, June 30, 1978.

Berchan, R. *The Inner Stage: An Essay on the Conflict of Vocations in the Early Works of Paul Claudel*. East Lansing, MI: Michigan State University Press, 1966.

Bradbury, M. "Fictions." Review of *At the Edge*. Quill & Quire, 40:4 (April 1974);20.

Burke, H. "His Name John Thompson." *Germination* 8:1 (Spring-Summer 1984): 40-43; and *Germination* 8:2 (Fall-Winter 1984): 43-48.

Char, R. *Oeuvres Complètes*. Paris: Gallimard, 1983.

Coles, D. "Words of a Different Sound." *Globe & Mail*, January 5, 1974.

Cooper, A. " 'Way back the woods are wine-dark': The Poetry of John Thompson." *Arts Atlantic* 17 (Summer 1983): 38-39.

Cooper, A. "I Must Write the Poem." *Antigonish Review* 42 (Summer 1980): 91-98.

Douglas, K. *Complete Poems*. Edited by D. Graham. London: Oxford University Press, 1978.

Fetherling, D. *Travels by Night: A Memoir of the Sixties*. Toronto: Lester, 1994.

Firmage, G.J., ed. *A Garland for Dylan Thomas*. New York: Clarke & Way, 1963.

Gasparini, L. "New Poet, New Fertility." *Windsor Star*, December 1, 1973.

Gibbs, R. "Almost Without Speech." *Fiddlehead* 104 (Winter 1975): 134-137.

Gibson, S.M. "Tantramar Poems." *Tamarack Review* 80 (Spring 1980): 72-82.

Gibson, S.M. *I Am Watching*. Toronto: Anansi, 1973.

Giguère, R. *L'Âge de la Parole: Poèmes 1949-1960*. Ottawa: Éditions de l'Hexagone, 1971.

Graham, D. *Keith Douglas, 1920-1944*. London: Oxford University Press, 1974.

Hall, P. "Posthumous Poetry: The Duty's a Pleasure." *Windsor Star*, August 19, 1978.

Harrison, J. *Outlyer and Ghazals*. New York: Simon and Shuster, 1971.

Jones, D.G. "Imperfect Ghazals." In *A Throw of Particles*. Toronto: General, 1983.

Keeney Smith, P. "Hit and Miss." Review of *At the Edge* and *Stilt Jack*. *Canadian Literature* (Summer 1980): 136-140.

Keyes, S. *The Collected Poems*. London: Routledge and Kegan Paul, 1945.

Lapointe, P-M. *Le Réel Absolu: Poèmes 1948-1963*. Ottawa: Éditions de l'Hexagone, 1971.

Lee, D. "The New Poets: Fresh Voices in the Land." *Saturday Night* 88:12 (December 1973): 33-35.

Levenson, C. "*At the Edge of the Chopping There Are No Secrets*." Review. *Penny Press* (Ottawa, n.d.).

Levenson, C. "Poetry and Fiction." *Queen's Quarterly* 86:4 (1979): 718-720.

Levertov, D. *O Taste and See*. New York: New Directions, 1964.

Lewis, A. *Ha! Ha! Among the Trumpets*. London: George Allen and Unwin, 1945.

Lochhead, D. "John Thompson." In *Upper Cape Poems*. Fredericton: Goose Lane, 1989.

Lochhead, D. *High Marsh Road*. Toronto: Anson-Cartwright, 1980.

M., A. "Poems Oblique, Head-On." *Victoria Times*, November 24, 1973.

Mathews, D.J. and C. Shackle, eds. and trans. *An Anthology of Classical Urdu Love Lyrics*. London: Oxford University Press, 1972.

Matthews, J. et al., eds. and trans. *Hypnos Waking: Selected Poems and Prose of René Char*. New York: Random House, 1956.

Mellor, D., ed. *A Paradise Lost: The Neo-Romantic Imagination in Britain, 1935-55*. London: Lund Humphries, 1987.

Nause, J. "Rural Imagery, Terrifying Fantasy." *Ottawa Journal*, August 10, 1974.

Norris, K. "Land Eels and Illogical Ghazals." *Books in Canada* (August-September 1978): 20-21.

Nowlan, A. "A Postcard to a Ghost." *Toronto Life* (December 1979): 222.

Ondaatje, M. *Secular Love*. Toronto: Coach House, 1984.

Polk, J. "Yeats. Yeats. Yeats. Yeats. Yeats," *Brick* 41 (Summer 1991): 66-70.

Press, J. *Rule & Energy: Trends in British Poetry Since the Second World War*. London: Oxford University Press, 1963.

Reaney, J.S. "Weaving Works into Continuous Whole Links These Poets." *London Free Press*, September 16, 1978.

Riley, J. *The Collected Works*. Leeds: Grosseteste, 1980.

Roethke, T. *Selected Letters*. Edited and introduced by R.J. Mills, Jr. Seattle: University of Washington Press, 1968.

Sanger, P. "John Thompson." In *The Oxford Companion to Twentieth-Century Poetry in English*. Edited by I. Hamilton. Oxford: Oxford University Press, 1994.

Sanger, P. "John Thompson: *Stilt Jack*: A Review." *Germination* 3:2 (Winter 1978): 36-37.

Sanger, P. *Sea Run: Notes on John Thompson's Stilt Jack*. Antigonish, N.S.: Xavier (*Antigonish Review*), 1986.

Schimanski, S. and H. Treece, eds. *A New Romantic Anthology*. London: Grey Walls, 1949.

Seager, A. *The Glass House: The Life of Theodore Roethke*. New York: McGraw-Hill, 1968.

Sears, W. "Mount 'A' Students Feel Professor Should Be Retained by University." *Saint John Telegraph-Journal*, April 6, 1970.

Smith, A.J.M. Interview by R. Jansma. *Red Cedar Review* 7:3-4 (July 1971): 44-49.

Sorestad, G. *"At the Edge of the Chopping There Are No Secrets."* Review. *Skylark* (Fall 1974)

Virgo, S. *"Stilt Jack*: A Review." *Quill & Quire* 44:10 (July 5, 1978):11.

Webb, P. "Review of *Sea Run: Notes on John Thompson's Stilt Jack*." *Canadian Literature* 100 (Spring 1987): 156-157.

Webb, P. *Sunday Water: 13 anti ghazals*. Victoria: Morris Printing, 1982.

Yeats, W.B. *Collected Poems*. London: Macmillan, 1973.

Yeats, W.B. *The Autobiography*. New York: Doubleday, 1958.

ACKNOWLEDGEMENTS

At the Edge of the Chopping There Are No Secrets, by John Thompson, was published by The House of Anansi Press in 1973; *Stilt Jack*, by John Thompson, was published by The House of Anansi Press in 1978. The poems from these books are reprinted with the permission of Stoddart Publishing Co. Limited, Don Mills, Ontario.

Translations of the following poems from *Oeuvres Complètes de René Char* (Bibliothèque de la Pléiade © Éditions Gallimard 1983) appear with the permission of Éditions Gallimard: "Homme-oiseau Mort et Bison Mourant," "Les Cerfs Noirs," "La Bête Innommable," "Jeune Cheval à la Crinière Vaporeuse," "Fièvre de la Petite-Pierre d'Alsace," "La Passe de Lyon," "La Lisière du Trouble," "Marmonnement," "Le Risque et le Pendule," "Pour Renouer," "Rapport de Marée," "Invitation," "La Bibliothèque est en Feu," "Les Compagnons dans le Jardin," "À Deux Enfants," "La Passante de Sceaux," "Épitaphe," "L'Arbre Frappé," "Neuf Merci," "Les Palais et les Maisons," "Dans l'Espace," "C'est Bien Elle," "La Grille," "Les Dieux sont de Retour," "Artine dans l'Écho," "Berceuse pour Chaque Jour jusqu'au Dernier," "Aux Miens," "La Fauvette des Roseaux," "Débris Mortels et Mozart," "L'Une et l'Autre," "Auguillon," "Sur une Nuit sans Ornement," "Attenants," "Captifs," "L'Oiseau Spirituel," "Ligne de Foi," "L'Issue," "Le Pas Ouvert de René Crevel," "Pour un Prométhée Saxifrage," "L'Escalier de Flore," "La Route par les Sentiers," "Déclarer son Nom," "Traverse," "Si . . . ," "De 1943," "La Faux Relevée," "L'Avenir non Prédit," "Éros Suspendu," "Nous Tombons," "La Montée de la Nuit," "Quitter," "Nous Avons," "Dans la Marche," "Éternité à Lourmarin," "Aux Riverains de la Sorgue," "Contrevenir," "Les Dentelles de Montmirail," "L'Allégresse," "Fontis," "Devancier," "Aux Portes d'Aerea," "Lied du Figuier," "Célébrer Giacometti," "Les Parages d'Alsace," "Mirage des Aiguilles," "Le Nu Perdu," "Chérir Thouzon," "La Soif Hospitalière," "Tracée sur le Gouffre," "Le Gaucher," "Avec Braque, peut-être, on s'était dit . . . ," "L'Âge Cassant."

The translation of "Rougeur des Matinaux," from *Oeuvres Complètes de René Char*, appears with the permission of Éditions Gallimard and Bloodaxe Books.

Translations of "La Vie Dévisagée," "Vivre Mieux," and "Continuer à Vivre," by Roland Giguère, and "Courtes Pailles," by Paul-Marie Lapointe, appear with permission of Éditions de l'Hexagone.

Without the help and encouragement of the following people, this book could not have been made. I have spoken to or corresponded with most of them. By the time I started work, the others had already circulated information or primary source material among the community of those who value

Thompson's work and memory. I am most grateful to the late Herbert Burke, Alan Bishop, R.D. Wayne Tompkins, Ross Galbraith, Lorne Bell, Akis Patapiou, Nick deVos and Allan Cooper. Cheri Croft-Wilson and Tim Crawford, particular early and constant friends of Thompson's, generously shared crucial information and provided photographs. Wayne Foley, former Chief of Police of Sackville, now retired, remembered details about the final month of Thompson's life for which little documentation has survived. Thompson liked Foley very much, would visit him for conversation and gave him a typescript of his poems. Carrie Macmillan, Michael Thorpe, Sara Lochhead and Thaddeus Holownia, all members of the faculty at Mount Allison University, helped to find some biographical details. So also did Carol Richardson of the Sackville Municipal Office. Marcia McConnell, Assistant Registrar, and Stefanie Wesley, Associate Registrar, at Michigan State University sent details concerning Thompson's years as a graduate student. Robert Quartell, Humanities and Social Sciences Librarian at Michigan State University Libraries, discovered many of the Michigan poems, cued by minimal information. Jett Whitehead, of Bay City, Michigan, my friend and a very fine dealer in rare books, found a Thompson poem I would otherwise have missed and obtained for me a copy of Berchan's book on Claudel. Another friend, Jean-Marc Cournac of Bourgoin, gave me material about René Char. At the University of Sheffield, Roger Allum, Director of the Public Relations Office, and Elizabeth O'Brien, of the Alumni Office, found biographical details which were crucial for an adequate account of Thompson's life in England. Liz O'Brien's enthusiastic faxes and letters and her successful, energetic pursuit of more information than Sheffield University's records contain were among the pleasures researching brought. Another was the continuous support given by Douglas Lochhead. He nurtured this edition through nearly five years of planning, editing and negotiation. Susanne Alexander, Laurel Boone, Brenda Berry, Julie Scriver and others of Goose Lane Editions kindly managed a dream for which they assumed responsibility. Nancy Minard and Karen Smith of Special Collections, the Killam Memorial Library, Dalhousie University, helped look for Thompson's work in Canadian publications and made comments about him which I have used. Bonnie Waddell, Head Librarian of the MacRae Library, Nova Scotia Agricultural College, gave wise advice and made several fruitful literature searches. John Townsend of Schooner Books and John Doull of Doull's Books, both in Halifax, and Jim Tillotson of The Odd Book in Wolfville had, as usual, the right books at the right time. The generosity and courage of George and Gertrude Sanderson and Frank Macdonald of *The Antigonish Review* enabled me to publish earlier research on Thompson's *Stilt Jack*. To Carol Ann Wooley (again) and Sandra Murphy (again), who together took the manuscript of this edition through many typescript versions, I offer deepest thanks for their ability, patience and friendship. As for my own work, it is dedicated as always to the mountain ash tree.

JOHN THOMPSON

280

INDEX

Index

Index

Index
287